Good Housekeeping
Cook's Year

Winter
KITCHEN

Good Housekeeping
Cook's Year

Winter
KITCHEN

DELICIOUS RECIPES AND
SEASONAL IDEAS FOR WINTER
COOKING AND ENTERTAINING

EBURY PRESS
LONDON

First published in 1997

1 3 5 7 9 10 8 6 4 2

First published in the United Kingdom in 1997 by Ebury Press
Random House, 20 Vauxhall Bridge Road, London, SW1V 2SA

Random House Australia (Pty) Limited
20 Alfred Street, Milsons Point, Sydney
New South Wales 2061, Australia

Random House New Zealand Limited
18 Poland Road, Glenfield,
Auckland 10, New Zealand

Random House South Africa (Pty) Limited
Endulini, 5a Jubilee Road,
Parktown, 2193, South Africa

Random House UK Limited Reg. No. 954009

A CIP catalogue record for this book is available from the British Library.

ISBN 0 09 185368 0

Managing Editor: Julia Canning
Design: Sara Kidd

Contributing authors: Jacqueline Clark, Maxine Clark, Joanna Farrow,
Jane Newdick, Louise Pickford, Louise Steel, Caroline Richmond Walker
Contributing editors: Helen Southall, Donna Wood
Additional research and assistance: Hilary Bird, Fiona Hunter, Sara Lewis
Recipe testing: Emma-Lee Gow, Patricia Stone

Special photography: Ken Field, Michelle Garrett, Graham Kirk
Photgraphic styling: Michelle Garrett, Roisin Nield, Helen Payne
Food for photography: Maxine Clark, Jane Newdick, Louise Pickford,
Liz Trigg, Joanna Farrow
Colour illustrations: Madeleine David

Printed and bound in Portugal by Printer Portuguesa, Lisbon

**The material in this book was previously published in
Good Housekeeping Cook's Year**

CONTENTS

COOKERY NOTES

- Both metric and imperial measures are given for the recipes. Follow either metric or imperial throughout as they are not interchangeable.

- All spoon measures are level unless otherwise stated. Sets of measuring spoons are available in metric and imperial for accurate measurements of small quantities.

- Ovens should be preheated to the temperature specified. Grills should be preheated. The cooking times given in the recipes assume that this has been done.

- Where a stage is specified in brackets under freezing, the dish should be frozen at the end of that stage.

- Large eggs should be used except where otherwise specified.

- Use freshly ground black pepper unless otherwise specified.

- Use fresh rather than dried herbs unless dried herbs are suggested in the recipes.

- Stocks should be freshly made if possible. Alternatively, buy ready-made stocks or use good quality stock cubes.

AT-A-GLANCE SYMBOLS

❋   The recipes can be frozen.

🕐   The recipes can be prepared and cooked in 30 minutes or under.

♡   The recipe is under 350 calories per portion for main courses and under 200 calories for starters, accompaniments and desserts.

WITH THE ARRIVAL of the first frosts of winter, the cook naturally turns to comforting and sustaining dishes to help keep out the chill. Hearty casseroles, packed with seasonal root vegetables, and warming hot puddings are the order of the day. As Christmas approaches, the festive spirit takes over - now's the time to make exciting party food and Christmas treats. This creativity in the kitchen culminates in the grand turkey feast - one of the highlights of a busy season for the cook. The pages that follow provide a superb guide for the winter kitchen, with seasonal decorating ideas as well as delicious and imaginative recipes using the best that the season has to offer.

To compensate for the cold and unfriendly weather outside, this is the time for warming, hearty food - dishes to comfort you through the chilly days and to bring a touch of warmth to the long, dark evenings.

Winter is also the season of giving and generosity, a time when family and friends get together to share food and drink in celebration of Christmas and the arrival of the New Year. So party food is definitely on the menu, too!

WINTER VEGETABLES

The seasonal vegetables are filling and nourishing, ideal for hearty bakes, roasts and casseroles.

Cabbages

Cabbages are at their best - Savoy cabbage is enjoyed for its bright colour and clean earthy flavour, while red cabbage adds texture and colour to satisfying casseroles. Curly kale, long neglected, is quite wonderful in thick soups or served as a vegetable dish, cooked lightly and tossed with lots of butter and black pepper.

Brussels Sprouts

Brussels sprouts are at their peak and provide the traditional accompaniment to the Christmas turkey. Take care not to overcook them - boil in salted water for 8-10 minutes until tender but still retaining their bite; or steam for about 15 minutes.
• For a tasty side dish, try tossing the hot, cooked sprouts in a dressing made with lemon juice and olive oil, flavoured with grated lemon rind, mustard and chopped parsley. Serve at once.
• For a nutty butter to serve with 1.4 kg (3 lb) Brussels sprouts, beat 75 g (3 oz) chopped toasted hazelnuts into 75 g (3 oz) softened unsalted butter, together with salt, pepper, nutmeg, 1 clove crushed garlic and the grated rind of 1 lemon.
• Top cooked sprouts with pieces of crisply-grilled streaky bacon and pared Parmesan cheese.

Root Vegetables

Traditional root vegetables, such as carrots, swedes, turnips, parsnips, Jerusalem artichokes and celeriac, are also at their prime at this time of year. They are delicious roughly mashed or finely puréed with butter or cream and plenty of salt, pepper, nutmeg or mace. Chopped fresh herbs add colour and flavour.

Sweet potatoes, especially the orange variety, make a great addition to stews, and are delicious roasted with sweet root vegetables such as parsnips

and carrots. They add a sweet nuttiness to mashed potato and are excellent puréed with fresh cooked chestnuts.

Try these easy ideas for seasonal root vegetables to give winter meals a lift.
• For extra-crunchy roast potatoes, parboil as usual, then toss in dried white breadrumbs and ground paprika before roasting. You will need 25 g (1 oz) breadcrumbs and a large pinch of paprika per 900 g (2 lb) potatoes.
• For glazed carrots with a difference, cook carrot sticks in boiling salted water for 5 minutes, then add halved kumquats (minus their pips). Cook for a further 5 minutes, then drain and toss in butter and pepper.
• Toss 700 g (1½ lb) cooked carrots or turnips in 15 ml (1 tbsp) clear honey with 15 ml (1 tbsp) lemon juice and sauté for 1 minute. Stir in 15 ml (1 tbsp) chopped fresh chives and plenty of seasoning.
• For creamed potato with celeriac, peel and slice 900 g (2 lb) potato and 450 g (1 lb) celeriac. Simmer in salted water with the juice of 1 lemon, for 25-30 minutes until tender, then mash. Return to a non-stick pan with 50 g (2 oz) butter, 30 ml (2 tbsp) milk and 30 ml (2 tbsp) roughly chopped watercress. Reheat, stirring all the time. Season and serve. This is delicious as a base for roast white fish fillets.
• Stir small cubes of Blue Brie into mashed potato a few minutes before serving.
• Slice root vegetables thinly and layer in a gratin dish, adding dots of butter between each layer. Pour in enough double cream and milk to cover, then season and bake at 180°C (350°F) mark 4 for about 1 hour until tender.

CHESTNUTS

Fresh chestnuts taste wonderful, but are time consuming to prepare. Try buying dried chestnuts from a good health-food shop or Italian delicatessen well before the festive season. These dried nuts are a great discovery - no boiling and peeling required, just cover with cold water and soak overnight, then use as described in a recipe.

Look out too for vacuum-packed ready-prepared chestnuts which come in tins and jars. These are expensive but handy if you are short of time.

Fresh Chestnuts

Fresh chestnuts only have a shelf life of one week, so buy near the day they are required, or prepare in advance, cook and freeze.

To peel chestnuts, make a tiny slit in the skin

near the pointed end, then cover with boiling water and leave for 5 minutes. Remove from the water, one at a time, and peel off the thick outer skin and thin inner skin while still warm.

To cook chestnuts, simmer the peeled nuts in unsalted water for 30-40 minutes. Alternatively, bake the nuts in their skins in the oven at 200°C (400°F) mark 6 for 20 minutes, then peel.

CITRUS FRUIT

Citrus fruits are abundant during the winter season, ranging from easy-peel and seedless varieties to new cross-varieties. They make a refreshing finish to a hearty winter meal.

January is the month for making marmalade with Seville oranges (see recipe page 73). Seville oranges make the clearest, sharpest marmalade and are in season in January and February. If you are pressed for time, freeze the oranges for making marmalade at a later date.

CHRISTMAS PLANNING

Christmas is the main festivity of this season. If you are entertaining, remember that you will need to

A traditional meal of succulent roast turkey with all the trimmings is, for many, the high spot of Christmas Day.

make the Christmas cake (see page 68) and the pudding (see page 62) ahead of time. To make life easier, you can also make some of the accompaniments well in advance. For instance, Bread Sauce, one of the traditional accompaniments to turkey, freezes well. Here are two more ideas for advance preparation.

Cranberry and apple relish This relish is an excellent accompaniment to roast turkey and can be made a week in advance. Peel, core and slice 350 g (12 oz) cooking apples. Place in a large saucepan with 225 g (8 oz) cranberries, 30 ml (2 tbsp) cider vinegar, 225 g (8 oz) demerara sugar, 2.5 ml (½ tsp) ground mixed spice and the grated rind of 1 orange. Simmer for 20 minutes or until the fruit is pulpy, stirring occasionally. Cool, cover and refrigerate for up to 1 week.

Whisky butter Whisky butter makes a delicious alternative to the traditional brandy butter for serving with Christmas pudding. Cream 125 g (4 oz) softened unsalted butter with 125 g (4 oz) light muscovado sugar until light and fluffy. Gradually beat in the grated rind and juice of 1 small orange, 1.25 ml (¼ tsp) mixed spice, a pinch of ground green cardamom and 45 ml (3 tbsp) whisky. Spoon into a container, cover tightly and freeze or store in the refrigerator.

ROAST TURKEY

The main course of a traditional Christmas meal is turkey. Buy free-frange if possible, but if a frozen bird is your only option, make sure that the bird is thoroughly thawed before cooking. Leave the frozen turkey in the bag and thaw at cool room temperature, not in the refrigerator. Remove the giblets as soon as they are loose to make stock for the gravy. To ensure that the bird is completely thawed, check that there are no ice crystals in the cavity and that the legs are quite flexible. Cook as soon as possible, once thawed.

Stuffing

Roast turkey is not complete without a good stuffing. As a general rule, allow about 225 g (8 oz) stuffing for each 2.3 kg (5 lb) dressed weight of bird and stuff just before cooking.
Classic chestnut stuffing For a 4.5-5.4 kg (9-12 lb) turkey. Mix 225 g (8 oz) pork sausagemeat with 225 g (8 oz) fresh brown breadcrumbs, 5 ml (1 tsp) fresh or dried thyme and salt and pepper. Roughly chop 440 g (15½ oz) can drained chestnuts, or 450 g (1 lb) peeled and cooked fresh chestnuts. Stir into the meat mixture. Place in a freezerproof container and freeze. To use, thaw and loosely stuff the neck end of the turkey only. Sew up the neck skin or use skewers to secure in place.

Gravy

Turkey gravy is all important. With so many trimmings you need a really tasty gravy to moisten the meat. If possible, make turkey stock from the giblets. Otherwise, make chicken stock in advance and reduce by half to increase the flavour.
• To make perfect gravy, lift the cooked turkey onto a warmed serving dish. Pour any liquid from the foil back into the tin. Tilt the tin to run the liquid into one corner. Spoon off all but 30 ml (2 tbsp) of the liquid fat, leaving the turkey juices behind. Place the tin over a low heat and add 30 ml (2 tbsp) flour. Stir in with a wooden spoon and cook for 1-2 minutes. Do not worry if it is lumpy at this stage. Slowly stir in 600 ml (1 pint) chicken or turkey stock. Bring to the boil, then simmer for 3-4 minutes or until the gravy is smooth and thin; whisk if necessary to make it quite smooth. Off the heat, add 30 ml (2 tbsp) dry sherry and season to taste. Strain into a warmed gravy boat and serve at once with the roast turkey.

CHRISTMAS GIFTS

Homemade food gifts will be much more appreciated than shop-bought presents, especially if they are gift-wrapped in pretty boxes or presented in glamorous twists of brightly coloured cellophane.

Chocolate Truffles

Chocolate truffles are rich and indulgent. Grate 225 g (8 oz) bitter, plain or milk chocolate into a small saucepan and add 75 ml (3 fl oz) double cream. Melt over a gentle heat, stir well, remove from the heat and cool to room temperature to thicken. Beat in 45 ml (3 tbsp) brandy, rum, orange liqueur, coffee liqueur, coconut liqueur or vanilla essence, then beat for about 5 minutes with an electric mixer until the mixture is light and fluffy and paler in colour. The mixture should stand in peaks when ready. Cover and chill until quite firm.

Sprinkle a tray with cocoa powder and place even-sized teaspoonfuls of truffle mixture on the tray. Dust your hands with a little cocoa powder and quickly roll the mixture into balls – make sure your hands are cool. Alternatively, roll in chopped nuts, chocolate vermicelli or grated chocolate. Place on waxed paper and refrigerate. The truffles can also be dipped in melted white or dark chocolate – freeze overnight before dipping.

These truffles will keep for about 4 days in the refrigerator. If giving them as a gift, don't forget to enclose a card with the 'eat by' details clearly marked!

Scented Sugars

Useful for adding delicate flavour to baked goods and desserts, scented sugars make excellent Christmas gifts. Simply choose from the flavourings given below and pack into attractive glass jars. Decorate with colourful ribbons.
• For vanilla sugar, split a half vanilla pod and bury in 225 g (8 oz) caster or granulated sugar.
• For spiced sugar, add 1 cinnamon stick, 2 cloves and 1 blade of mace to the sugar.
• For lavender sugar, use 5 ml (1 tsp) dried lavender heads in the sugar.
• For citrus sugar, dry the pared rind of 1 orange and 1 lemon in the lowest oven for about 40 minutes. Cool and add to the sugar.

Candied Peel

Candied peel is easy to make but the standing time is spread over 4-5 days. It is infinitely superior to bought peel and is much cheaper!

Scrub clean 2 oranges and 2 lemons and pat dry. Cut into quarters and remove the peel, then cut into strips, if wished. Simmer the peel in enough water to cover for 1½-2 hours until tender, topping up with boiling water. Add 50 g (2 oz) sugar per fruit, stir to dissolve and bring to the boil. Leave uncovered for 24 hours. Re-boil and simmer for 4 minutes and leave uncovered for another 24 hours. Bring to the boil again and simmer until almost all the syrup is absorbed. Drain and lay on a wire rack placed over greaseproof paper.

Dry in an airing cupboard for 2-3 days until no longer sticky. You can speed up this process by placing in a 110°C (225°F) mark ¼ oven for 12 hours, turning occasionally.

Pack between waxed paper in a cardboard box – do not use an airtight container otherwise the fruit may turn mouldy. Candied peel will keep for about 6 months.

Lovely gifts for Christmas – scented sugars, candied peel and rich Bûche de Noël (see page 70).

Chocolate Fudge

Easy to make and quite irresistible, fudge is a perfect Christmas gift. Place 450 g (1 lb) sugar in a large heavy-based saucepan with 150 ml (5 fl oz) milk, 150 g (5 oz) butter, 150 g (5 oz) plain chocolate and 50 g (2 oz) honey. Heat gently, stirring, until the sugar has dissolved. Bring to the boil without stirring, then continue boiling until a temperature of 115°C (240°F) is reached on a sugar thermometer, stirring occasionally. Stand on a cool surface for 5 minutes, then beat until thick and beginning to 'grain'. Pour into a lightly oiled 18 cm (7 inch) shallow square tin; mark into squares when almost set. Cut when cold.

• For vanilla fudge, reduce the butter to 75 g (3 oz) and use 175 g (6 oz) can evaporated milk instead of the chocolate and honey. Boil as above, then remove from the heat, add 2.5 ml (½ tsp) vanilla essence and beat until thick. Pour into the tin and mark into squares.

11

GINGERBREAD CASKET

A little treasure chest made of gingerbread is a novel twist on a traditional gingerbread house. It also makes an original way of serving biscuits, sweets or nuts.

For a shiny finish, brush the dough with egg white before baking. The casket is held together with royal icing. Either use chocolate icing or tint white icing with brown food colouring.

Gingerbread is traditionally decorated with cloves. Painted with edible gold paint after baking, they give the chest a realistic studded look.

You will need:
1 quantity of Craft Gingerbread dough (see below)
Thin card for templates
Large sharp knife
Non-stick baking parchment
Baking sheets
Cloves and star anise
Brown royal icing
Icing bag
Gold tassel and wooden stick

CRAFT GINGERBREAD

Place 175 g (6 oz) soft brown sugar in a saucepan with 60 ml (4 tbsp) golden syrup, 30 ml (2 tbsp) black treacle, 30 ml (2 tbsp) water, 5 ml (1 tsp) grated nutmeg and 10 ml (2 tsp) each ground cinnamon and ginger. Heat gently until sugar has melted. Remove from the heat, add 200 g (7 oz) butter and 5 ml (1 tsp) bicarbonate of soda, then stir in 450 g (1 lb) plain flour to make a stiff dough. Turn out and knead into a ball and leave to cool for 1 hour. Roll out.

1 Cut templates for two sides 11 x 8 cm ($4^{1}/_{2}$ x $3^{1}/_{4}$ inches), a front and back 16 x 8 cm ($6^{1}/_{2}$ x $3^{1}/_{4}$ inches), a base 16 x 12 cm ($6^{1}/_{2}$ x $4^{3}/_{4}$ inches) and a lid 16 x 14 cm ($6^{1}/_{2}$ x $5^{1}/_{2}$ inches). Also cut two arched sides pieces for lid. Lay on the rolled-out dough and cut around.

2 Transfer the dough pieces to lined baking sheets. Allow room for spreading. Decorate with cloves and star anise. Bake at 180°C (350°F) mark 4 until just cooked and lightly browned.

3 Trim the edges while still warm, using the templates as a guide. Immediately place the lid on a curved surface to dry.

4 When the pieces are cold, assemble the casket – pipe royal icing along the edges and stick together, supporting the pieces until set. Attach a gold tassel to the lid with icing. Prop the lid open on a wooden stick.

GIFT-WRAPPED SWEETS

Fancy wrappings make the simplest gift look outstanding. Here inexpensive sweets and chocolates are wrapped up in stylish cellophane and presented in pretty boxes.

Look out for transparent cellophane in iridescent colours to bundle up sugared almonds, marshmallows or Turkish Delight. Tie up the little parcels with dainty ribbons to complement the colour theme. Save a collection of small boxes that can be re-lined or covered with giftwrap or handmade paper to hold sweets or chocolates.

You will need:
**Small boxes, covered or
  uncovered
Giftwrap or handmade papers
  for covering boxes
Shallow basket
Shredded tissue paper
Metallic foil paper
White paper
Selection of sweets, such as
  Turkish Delight, marshmallow
  twists, sugared almonds in
  silver, white, turquoise and
  pink
Cellophane
White chocolate truffles
Soft, gauzy ribbon
Leaf-print labels**

• Cover and line small boxes with giftwrap or handmade papers.
• To line a small round box, cut a band of thin white paper, twice as long as its circumference and slightly deeper than the sides, fold it concertina fashion and fit it round the inside of the box. Trim the collar into zigzag points to make a decorative edging.
• Cut circles or squares of cellophane and pile a few sugared almonds into the centre.

Tie the bundles up tightly at the top with ribbon and arrange them in a pretty box or shallow basket to give as a present.
• Line a basket with shredded tissue paper, then arrange chocolate truffles on top. Tie a big ribbon bow on the handle or around the rim.
• Wind a wide ribbon around a box with a lid and tie it off in a large bow.
• Attach labels to perishable sweets and chocolates, such as fresh cream truffles, giving an eat-by date.

CHRISTMAS MARZIPAN TREE

A little Christmas tree decorated with marzipan fruits and colourful baubles forms a cheerful centrepiece for a Christmas dinner table or on a window sill. The tree lasts particularly well when it is made from sprigs of blue spruce.

The fruits are modelled from either bought or homemade coloured marzipan and are so easy to make that children can have great fun helping to make them. You can choose a colour scheme that fits in with the other decorations in the room.

You will need:
**Pink, green, white and yellow
  marzipan
Cloves
Wooden kebab sticks
Pot to stand the tree in
Green florist's foam
Plastic-coated wire netting
Paper for template
Secateurs or wire cutters
Stiff florist's wires
1 wooden houseplant stake
Branch of blue spruce
Christmas tree baubles**

1 Mould the marzipan into fruit. Press cloves into the fruit as stems and calyces. Leave to dry, then spear onto sticks.

3 Pack the pot with foam and push in the pyramid stake. Cut sprigs of spruce and stick into pyramid to make a conical tree.

2 Cut pieces of foam to stack into a pyramid. Using a template, trim wire netting into a cone. Wrap around the foam and push in central stake.

4 When the tree is complete, push the sticks of fruits into the foam. Then tie the baubles onto the tree, spacing them evenly among the fruit.

PLAITED BREAD RING

A circular bread plait, baked until a rich golden brown, makes a lovely base for a ring of candles. The invitingly edible looking plait makes a particularly good dinner-table decoration, adding soft lines and golden tones to the table setting. The candles, with their defined shape, stand out strikingly against the natural curves of the plait, while the flickering flames enhance the mellow colouring of the bread crust.

Bread dough is excellent for modelling, being very flexible when raw and easy to carve into once baked. It's also surprisingly simple to make - just follow the bread recipe on page 76, up to stage 3.

You will need:
3 quantity Wholemeal Bread dough (see page 76)
Small pointed knife
Pastry brush
Apple corer
Beaten egg for glazing
8-10 white candles

1 Cut off one quarter of the kneaded dough and reserve for the decoration. Divide the remaining dough into three and shape into long rolls, making sure they are the same length.
2 Pinch the rolls together at one end and plait loosely. Shape into a ring and pinch the ends together.
3 Make the 'bunch of grapes' decoration using the reserved

dough. Roll small balls to represent the grapes and cut out simple, flat leaf shapes. Arrange the decorations in groups on the dough, sticking them in place by brushing the dough with water.
4 Cut holes for the candles with an apple corer. Brush the ring with beaten egg to glaze.
5 Bake the ring at 220° C (425° F) mark 7 for 20 minutes. Reduce the temperature to 180° C (350° F) mark 4 and bake for a further 15 minutes.
6 While still warm, trim the holes to fit the candles. When cold, slot the candles in place.
7 Remember to watch out that the candles do not burn down too far.

JERUSALEM ARTICHOKE AND PARMESAN SOUP

PREPARATION TIME 15 minutes
COOKING TIME 25 minutes
FREEZING Suitable
♡ ❄

SERVES 6
- *50 g (2 oz) butter*
- *2 shallots, peeled and diced*
- *5 ml (1 tsp) mild curry paste*
- *450 g (1 lb) Jerusalem artichokes, scrubbed clean and thinly sliced*
- *900 ml (1½ pints) chicken or vegetable stock*
- *150 ml (5 fl oz) single cream (or milk for a less rich soup)*
- *freshly grated nutmeg, to taste*

190 CALS/SERVING
- *pinch of cayenne pepper*
- *60 ml (4 tbsp) freshly grated Parmesan cheese*
- *salt and pepper*
PARMESAN TOAST
- *3-4 slices day-old softgrain white bread*
- *a little freshly grated Parmesan cheese, for sprinkling*
- *1.25 ml (¼ tsp) paprika*

1 Melt the butter in a large saucepan and add the shallots. Cook gently for 5 minutes until soft and golden. Stir in the curry paste and cook for 1 minute. Add the sliced artichokes and stock; stir well. Bring to the boil, cover and simmer for about 15 minutes or until the artichokes are tender.

2 Meanwhile, make the Parmesan toast. Toast the bread lightly on both sides. Quickly cut off the crusts and split each slice in two. Scrape off any doughy bits, then sprinkle with Parmesan and paprika. Place on a baking sheet and bake in the oven at 180ºC (350ºF) mark 4 for 10-15 minutes or until uniformly golden.

3 Add the cream, nutmeg and cayenne to the soup. Transfer to a blender or food processor and work until smooth, then pass through a sieve into a clean saucepan. Reheat the soup and stir in the Parmesan cheese. Taste and adjust the seasoning. Serve at once, with the hot toast.

VARIATION Replace the Jerusalem artichokes with 1 large cauliflower. Cut away the leaves and core, and discard. Divide the cauliflower into florets. Add to the shallots with the stock and bring to the boil. Simmer for about 10 minutes or until very soft, then continue as in stage 3.

CREAMY CARROT AND CELERIAC SOUP

PREPARATION TIME 15 minutes
COOKING TIME 45 minutes
FREEZING Suitable (stage 3)
♡ ❄

SERVES 6   200 CALS/SERVING

- *30 ml (2 tbsp) vegetable oil*
- *225 g (8 oz) onions, peeled and roughly chopped*
- *900 g (2 lb) carrots, peeled and roughly chopped*
- *900 g (2 lb) celeriac, peeled and roughly chopped*
- *1.7 litres (3 pints) chicken stock*
- *5 ml (1 tsp) soy sauce*
- *finely grated rind and juice of 1 orange*
- *300 ml (10 fl oz) single cream*
- *salt and pepper*
- *croûtons and flat-leaf parsley, to garnish*

1 Heat the oil in a large saucepan and add the vegetables. Sauté for 5 minutes, stirring frequently. Add the chicken stock and bring to the boil. Cover and then leave to simmer gently for 20 minutes.
2 Stir in the soy sauce, orange rind and 60 ml (4 tbsp) orange juice. Cover and simmer for 20 minutes.
3 Cool slightly, then blend in a food processor until smooth. For an extra-velvety texture, push through a sieve.
4 Stir in the cream and warm gently. Season to taste and serve garnished with croûtons and parsley.

SPICED DAL SOUP

PREPARATION TIME 10 minutes, plus soaking
COOKING TIME 1½ hours
FREEZING Suitable
♡ ❄

SERVES 4-6   200-130 CALS/SERVING

- *125 g (4 oz) yellow split peas*
- *5 ml (1 tsp) cumin seeds*
- *10 ml (2 tsp) coriander seeds*
- *3 dried red chillies*
- *15 ml (1 tbsp) desiccated unsweetened coconut*
- *30 ml (2 tbsp) ghee or vegetable oil*
- *225 g (8 oz) tomatoes, skinned and roughly chopped*
- *2.5 ml (½ tsp) ground turmeric*
- *5 ml (1 tsp) treacle*
- *5 ml (1 tsp) salt*
- *coriander sprigs and lemon slices, to garnish*

1 Put the split peas into a sieve and wash thoroughly under cold running water. Drain well, then transfer to a bowl, cover with cold water and soak for 8 hours. Drain, place in a large saucepan, cover with 600 ml (1 pint) water and boil rapidly for 10 minutes. Cover and simmer for at least 1 hour, or until tender.
2 Finely grind the cumin, coriander, chillies and coconut in a small electric mill or with a pestle and mortar. Heat the ghee or oil in a heavy-based frying pan, add the spice mixture and fry, stirring, for 30 seconds. Set aside.
3 Mash the split peas and transfer to a large saucepan. Stir in the tomatoes, fried spices, turmeric, treacle, salt and 300 ml (10 fl oz) water.
4 Bring to the boil, then lower the heat, cover and simmer for about 20 minutes. Taste and adjust the seasoning and turn into a warmed serving dish. Garnish with coriander sprigs and lemon slices.

TIP
Poppadoms make an excellent accompaniment to this soup. To cook poppadoms, either fry for a few seconds in vegetable oil or brush with oil and grill for a few seconds on each side.

LITTLE SPANISH SAVOURIES

PREPARATION TIME 30 minutes, plus pastry
COOKING TIME 10 minutes
FREEZING Suitable (stage 2)

❄

MAKES ABOUT 24
- 225 g (8 oz) Puff Pastry (see page 75)
- butter for greasing
- 125 g (4 oz) firm goats' cheese or mozzarella, diced
- 50 g (2 oz) sun-dried tomatoes in oil, drained and roughly chopped

65 CALS/SAVOURY
- 50 g (2 oz) capers, chopped
- 50 g (2 oz) can anchovy fillets, chopped
- 50 g (2 oz) pitted olives, quartered
- 50 g (2 oz) pesto sauce
- salt and pepper

1 Roll out the pastry to 3 mm (⅛ inch) thick. Stamp out 24 circles with a 5 cm (2 inch) cutter and place on a greased baking sheet.
2 Top with the cheese, sun-dried tomatoes, capers, anchovies and olives. Spoon pesto sauce over and season with salt and pepper.
3 Cook at 200°C (400°F) mark 6 for 10-15 minutes or until crisp. Serve hot.

NAN BREAD WITH SPICY PRAWNS

PREPARATION TIME 20 minutes
COOKING TIME About 15 minutes
FREEZING Not suitable

MAKES ABOUT 60
- 15 ml (1 tbsp) vegetable oil
- 1 garlic clove, peeled and crushed
- 10 ml (2 tsp) mild curry powder
- 4 spring onions, finely chopped
- 350 g (12 oz) cooked peeled prawns, roughly chopped

25 CALS/SQUARE
- 20 ml (4 tsp) mango chutney
- 20 ml (4 tsp) natural yogurt
- salt and pepper
- 2 large nan bread, about 300 g (10 oz) total weight

1 Heat the oil in a frying pan and add the garlic, curry powder and onions. Cook for 1 minute, stirring, then add the prawns. Cook gently for a further 2-3 minutes. Off the heat, stir in the chutney and yogurt. Season to taste and set aside.
2 Heat the nan bread in the oven according to packet instructions, then cut into small squares and top with a little of the prawn mixture. Serve warm or cold.

SMOKED SALMON ROULADE

PREPARATION TIME 30 minutes, plus chilling
FREEZING Not suitable

MAKES 70 ROUNDS
- *1 large bunch watercress*
- *225 g (8 oz) full-fat soft cheese with garlic and herbs*
- *10 ml (2 tsp) lemon juice*

20 CALS/ROUND
- *black pepper*
- *225 g (8 oz) smoked salmon*
- *lemon wedges, to garnish*

1 Finely chop the watercress, discarding any coarse stalks. Using an electric whisk, mix the watercress into the soft cheese with the lemon juice and plenty of black pepper.
2 Cut out a piece of greaseproof paper measuring 30 x 33 cm (12 x 13 inches). Lay the pieces of smoked salmon on top, overlapping each piece slightly to form a rectangle of about 30 x 28 cm (12 x 11 inches). Cut in half widthways to make two rectangles.
3 Spread the soft-cheese mixture over both rectangles, then carefully roll each one into a thin sausage, using the paper to help you. Cover and refrigerate overnight.
4 Cut each roll into 5 mm (¼ inch) slices and serve immediately, garnished with wedges of lemon.

NUTTY CHICKEN BITES

PREPARATION TIME 40 minutes, plus marinating
COOKING TIME About 15 minutes
FREEZING Not suitable

MAKES ABOUT 70
- *900 g (2 lb) skinless chicken breast fillets*
- *125 g (4 oz) onion, peeled and finely chopped*
- *90 ml (6 tbsp) dark soy sauce*
- *50 ml (10 tsp) dark muscovado sugar*
DIP
- *15 ml (1 tbsp) vegetable oil*

115 CALS/ BITE WITH DIP
- *2 garlic cloves, peeled and crushed*
- *5 ml (1 tsp) mild curry powder*
- *10-15 ml (2-3 tsp) mild chilli powder*
- *450 g (1 lb) crunchy peanut butter*
- *pinch of salt*
- *½ cucumber*

1 Beat out the chicken breasts between sheets of greaseproof paper. Cut into 2.5 cm (1 inch) pieces.
2 Mix the onion with the soy sauce and 20 ml (4 tsp) sugar. Pour over the chicken and toss well. Cover and refrigerate overnight.
3 Meanwhile, make the dip. Heat the oil in a pan and add the garlic, curry and chilli powders. Cook for 1-2 minutes, then add the peanut butter, salt and remaining sugar with 450 ml (15 fl oz) water. Simmer for 5 minutes, stirring, until thick.
4 Thread the chicken onto cocktail sticks. Cook at 220°C (425°F) mark 7 for 10 minutes until cooked through. Cut the cucumber into 1 cm (½ inch) pieces and thread onto the sticks. Serve with the cold dip

VEGETABLE SAMOSAS

PREPARATION TIME 45 minutes, plus cooling
COOKING TIME About 35 minutes
FREEZING Suitable

❊

MAKES 24

- *450 g (1 lb) potatoes, peeled and halved*
- *salt and pepper*
- *15 ml (1 tbsp) vegetable oil*
- *1 onion, peeled and finely chopped*
- *1 garlic clove, peeled and crushed*
- *1-2 hot green chillies, deseeded and chopped*
- *10 ml (2 tsp) ground coriander*
- *10 ml (2 tsp) cumin seeds*
- *5 ml (1 tsp) ground fenugreek*
- *1 large ripe tomato, chopped*

150 CALS/SAMOSA

- *50 g (2 oz) frozen peas*
- *30 ml (2 tbsp) chopped fresh coriander*
- *15 ml (1 tbsp) chopped fresh mint*
- *oil for deep-frying*
- *mint sprigs and lime halves, to garnish*

PASTRY

- *450 g (1 lb) white plain flour*
- *5 ml (1 tsp) salt*
- *45 ml (3 tbsp) chopped fresh coriander (optional)*
- *60 ml (4 tbsp) vegetable oil, melted ghee or butter*

1 Cook the potatoes in boiling salted water until just tender. Drain and chop into fairly small pieces.

2 Heat the oil in a frying pan, add the onion and garlic and cook for about 5 minutes until softened. Add the spices and cook for 2 minutes, stirring continuously.

3 Add the tomato to the pan and simmer until softened. Add the potatoes and stir to coat in the spice mixture. Add the peas and cook for 1-2 minutes until thawed. Add the herbs and plenty of seasoning, then allow to cool.

4 To make the pastry, mix the flour with the salt and herbs, if using, in a bowl. Add the oil or melted fat and enough warm water to make a soft dough - about 200 ml (7 fl oz). Turn onto a lightly floured surface and knead for about 5 minutes.

5 Divide the dough into 12 pieces; keep covered with a damp cloth to prevent drying out. Roll one piece out to a 15 cm (6 inch) round and cut in half to make two semi-circles. Place a heaped teaspoon of filling on each semi-circle. Dampen the edges, fold over the filling and press together to seal. Repeat with the remaining pastry and filling.

6 Heat the oil in a deep-fat fryer to 180°C (350°F). Test the temperature by dropping a small piece of pastry into the oil - the pastry should sizzle immediately on contact and rise to the surface.

7 Deep-fry the samosas, about three at a time, for 3-5 minutes or until pale golden brown. Drain on crumpled absorbent kitchen paper. Serve warm, garnished with mint and lime halves.

VARIATION *Meat samosas* Omit the potato. After frying the spices, add 175 g (6 oz) minced lamb or beef and fry until browned. Add 5-10 ml (1-2 tsp) curry paste and a few spoonfuls of water, and cook for about 20 minutes or until the meat is tender. Add the peas and cook for 2 minutes. Cool and complete as above.

TIP
Make a quick chutney to accompany the samosas. Peel and finely slice a few spring onions, mix with a little crushed garlic, then toss with freshly torn mint and coriander leaves, a splash of lemon juice, a dash of oil and plenty of seasoning.

CARPACCIO OF SALMON

PREPARATION TIME 20 minutes
FREEZING Not suitable
♡ ⏱

SERVES 10
- *575 g (1¼ lb) salmon fillet, skinned*
- *125 ml (4 fl oz) olive oil*
- *225 g (8 oz) tomatoes, skinned, deseeded and finely chopped*
- *1 bunch fresh chives or spring onions, cut into long pieces*

200 CALS/SERVING
- *juice of 2 limes*
- *salt and pepper*
- *lime wedges, to garnish*
- *slices of brown bread and butter, to serve*

1 Cut the salmon into 20 slices. Bat out thinly between sheets of oiled clingfilm. It should be the thickness of sliced smoked salmon.
2 Mix the tomatoes and chives or spring onions with the lime juice, olive oil and seasoning.
3 Just before serving, arrange the salmon on individual serving plates and spoon the dressing over. Garnish with lime wedges and serve with slices of brown bread and butter.

VARIATION If the idea of eating raw salmon doesn't really appeal to you, serve the same quantity of sliced smoked salmon instead. Alternatively, place the thin salmon slices in single layers in ovenproof dishes and cook in the oven at 220°C (425°F) mark 7 for about 5 minutes or until the salmon just turns opaque. Serve warm, garnished with lime.

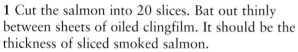

GRILLED PEPPER AND AUBERGINE SALAD

PREPARATION TIME 20 minutes
COOKING TIME 10 minutes
FREEZING Not suitable
♡ ⏱

SERVES 4
- *30 ml (2 tbsp) French dressing*
- *15 ml (1 tbsp) extra-virgin olive oil*
- *2 small, fat aubergines, cut into slices*
- *2 large, long red peppers*

120 CALS/SERVING
- *10 ml (2 tsp) lemon juice*
- *30 ml (2 tbsp) chopped fresh basil*
- *1 garlic clove, peeled and thinly sliced*
- *salt and pepper*
- *fresh basil leaves, to garnish*

1 Mix together the French dressing and olive oil. Brush the aubergine slices with the dressing mixture and then grill with the whole peppers until blackened all over, turning the aubergine slices and brushing with more dressing. Put them in a bowl and immediately cover with a damp tea towel. Leave until cool enough to handle.
2 Remove the charred skins from the peppers and cut lengthways into quarters, removing the core and seeds and reserving any juices in a bowl. Stir the remaining cooking juices from the grill pan into the bowl, then add the lemon juice, basil and garlic. Season with salt and pepper. Drizzle the mixture over the vegetables. Serve at room temperature, garnished with basil leaves.

FISH PLAKI WITH ROOT VEGETABLES

PREPARATION TIME 15 minutes, plus cooling
COOKING TIME 35-45 minutes
FREEZING Suitable
♡ ✳

SERVES 4

- 45 ml (3 tbsp) olive oil
- 2 onions, peeled and sliced
- 2 garlic cloves, peeled and crushed
- 2 carrots, peeled, halved lengthways and sliced
- 225 g (8 oz) celeriac, peeled and diced
- salt and pepper
- 3 plum tomatoes, skinned, deseeded and diced

290 CALS/SERVING

- 1 lemon, sliced
- 15 ml (1 tbsp) chopped fresh thyme
- 75 ml (3 fl oz) dry white wine
- 4 cod or tuna fish steaks, each weighing about 150 g (5 oz)
- 45 ml (3 tbsp) chopped fresh parsley, to garnish

1 Heat the oil in a large shallow saucepan, add the onions and cook over moderate heat for 5 minutes until softened and beginning to brown. Add the garlic, carrots and celeriac and cook for 8 minutes, stirring occasionally.

2 Stir in 150 ml (5 fl oz) water and season with salt and pepper to taste. Cover and simmer for 10-15 minutes, until the carrot and celeriac are very tender. Add the tomatoes, sliced lemon and thyme and simmer for 2-3 minutes. Add the wine.

3 Place the fish steaks in the sauce, cover and cook over a low heat for 10-15 minutes until the fish is cooked and flakes easily. Leave to cool for about 15 minutes, then sprinkle with the parsley to garnish and serve warm.

COD IN ORANGE AND CIDER SAUCE

PREPARATION TIME 15 minutes
COOKING TIME 25-30 minutes
FREEZING Suitable
♡ ✳

SERVES 4

- 4 cod fillets, skinned, each weighing about 175 g (6 oz)
- 1 orange
- 175 g (6 oz) onion, peeled and chopped
- black pepper
- 150 ml (5 fl oz) medium-dry cider

160 CALS/SERVING

- 125 ml (4 fl oz) fish stock
- 10 ml (2 tsp) chopped fresh coriander
- coriander sprigs and orange slices, to garnish

1 Place the fish in a 1.1 litre (2 pint) ovenproof dish. Pare the rind from the orange and cut into 7.5 cm (3 inch) long thin strips. Place on top of the fish with the onion and season with black pepper.

2 Mix 30 ml (2 tbsp) orange juice with the cider and fish stock. Pour over the fish, cover and bake in the oven at 190°C (375°F) mark 5 for 20-25 minutes or until the fish is cooked through.

3 Carefully place the onion, orange strips and fish in a serving dish and keep them warm.

4 Strain the cooking liquid into a small saucepan and boil rapidly for about 5 minutes or until the liquid is reduced by half. Pour over the fish and sprinkle with the coriander. Garnish with coriander sprigs and orange slices and serve immediately.

KEDGEREE WITH LENTILS

PREPARATION TIME 15 minutes
COOKING TIME About 45 minutes
FREEZING Not suitable
♡

SERVES 6

- *75 g (3 oz) green lentils, rinsed in cold water and drained*
- *450 g (1 lb) smoked haddock fillets*
- *300 ml (10 fl oz) milk*
- *1 onion, peeled and sliced*
- *175 g (6 oz) basmati or long-grain rice*
- *10 ml (2 tsp) coriander seeds*

305 CALS/SERVING

- *2 cloves*
- *2 cardamom pods*
- *15 ml (1 tbsp) vegetable oil*
- *finely grated rind and juice of 1 lime*
- *2 eggs, hard-boiled and cut into wedges*
- *chopped fresh coriander or parsley and lime slices, to garnish*

1 Put the lentils in a pan with enough cold water to cover generously. Bring to the boil and boil vigorously for 10 minutes, then simmer for about 15 minutes or until tender. Set on one side.

2 Meanwhile, put the smoked haddock into a wide saucepan, pour the milk over and add the onion. Bring to the boil and cook, covered, for 20-25 minutes, depending on the thickness of the fish, until the flesh flakes easily. Set on one side.

3 Rinse the rice several times in cold water to remove the starch.

4 Crush the coriander seeds, cloves and cardamom pods. Heat the oil in a large saucepan, and add the spices. Cook for 1 minute, then add the rice. Stir until the grains are coated in oil, then add 600 ml (1 pint) water. Bring to the boil and simmer gently, covered, for about 20 minutes, until the rice is tender.

5 Remove the fish skin and flake the flesh.

6 Add the lime juice and rind to the rice. Stir in the eggs. Drain the lentils and add to the rice with the fish. Reheat briefly, stirring. To serve, sprinkle with coriander or parsley and garnish with lime.

blended. Add the remaining spinach and blend.
Season to taste. Arrange the fish on plates, spoon
over the sauce and garnish with lime

FISH WITH LEMON AND GINGER

PREPARATION TIME 20 minutes, plus marinating
COOKING TIME 20-25 minutes
FREEZING Not suitable

♡

SERVES 6
- *5 ml (1 tsp) garam masala or curry powder*
- *5 cm (2 inch) piece fresh root ginger, peeled and finely chopped*
- *2 garlic cloves, peeled and crushed*
- *12 sole fillets, skinned, about 1.1 kg (2½ lb) total weight*
- *175 g (6 oz) spring onions, chopped*
- *45 ml (3 tbsp) chopped fresh coriander*

295 CALS/SERVING
- *finely grated rind and juice of 1 lemon*
- *salt and pepper*
- *50 g (2 oz) creamed coconut*
- *2.5 ml (½ tsp) saffron strands*
- *25 g (1 oz) salted cashew nuts*
- *15 ml (1 tbsp) vegetable oil*
- *150 ml (5 fl oz) single cream*
- *fresh coriander, spring onions and lime slices, to garnish*

1 Mix together the garam masala, ginger and
garlic. Place the sole fillets in a flat, non-metallic
dish and rub over with the spice mixture. Cover
tightly and marinate in the refrigerator overnight.
2 Mix half the spring onions with the coriander,
lemon rind, 45 ml (3 tbsp) lemon juice and
seasoning. Place the fillets, skinned-sides up, on a
plate and spoon a little of the onion mixture into
the centre of each one. Roll up and secure with a
cocktail stick.
3 In a food processor, blend the coconut, saffron
and cashew nuts with 200 ml (7 fl oz) water.
4 Heat the oil in a large shallow flameproof
casserole and fry the remaining spring onions for
2-3 minutes. Add the coconut liquid and fish with
any remaining marinade. Bring to the boil, cover
and simmer very gently for 15-20 minutes or until
the fish is cooked but still tender.
5 Add the cream and heat gently without boiling
for 2-3 minutes. Season, garnish and serve hot.

LEMON SOLE WITH SPINACH AND LIME HOLLANDAISE

PREPARATION TIME 15 minutes
COOKING TIME 20 minutes
FREEZING Not suitable

SERVES 4
- *oil for brushing*
- *4 lemon sole, each weighing 225 g (8 oz)*
- *45 ml (3 tbsp) wine vinegar*
- *4 black peppercorns*
- *4 egg yolks*
- *250 g (9 oz) unsalted butter, melted*

680 CALS/SERVING
- *10 ml (2 tsp) lime juice*
- *grated rind of ½ lime*
- *50 g (2 oz) young spinach leaves*
- *salt and pepper*
- *lime wedges, to garnish*

1 Lightly oil a baking tray. Place the fish on the
tray in a single layer, with the brown sides
uppermost. Brush with oil.
2 Place the fish under a hot grill, about 10-15 cm
(4-6 inches) from the heat source, and cook for
15-20 minutes, without turning.
3 Meanwhile, boil the vinegar and peppercorns in
a heavy-based saucepan until reduced to 22 ml
(1½ tbsp). Remove from the heat, then lift out
and discard the peppercorns. Place the egg yolks
in a blender and process for 1-2 minutes. Keeping
the machine running, add the reduced vinegar,
then very slowly add the hot melted butter, adding
at intervals the lime juice, lime rind and 30 ml
(2 tbsp) hot water.
4 Add half the spinach and process until well

NORMANDY SKATE WITH
CAPER SAUCE

PREPARATION TIME 5 minutes
COOKING TIME 15-20 minutes
FREEZING Not suitable
♡ ⏱

SERVES 4
- *4 pieces of skate wing, each weighing about 200 g (7 oz)*
- *1 celery stick*
- *2 shallots, peeled and roughly chopped*
- *2 bay leaves*
- *5 ml (1 tsp) black peppercorns*
- *75 ml (5 tbsp) cider vinegar*

330 CALS/SERVING
- *10 ml (2 tsp) capers, chopped*
- *150 ml (5 fl oz) double cream*
- *30 ml (2 tbsp) chopped fresh parsley*
- *salt and pepper*
- *parsley sprigs, to garnish*

1 Ask your fishmonger to skin the skate wings if necessary, and cut to the right portion size.
2 Break the celery stick into 3 or 4 pieces. Put them into a large saucepan with the shallots, bay leaves, peppercorns and 60 ml (4 tbsp) of the cider vinegar. Add 1.1 litres (2 pints) cold water, slide in the skate and slowly bring to just below the boil.
3 Cover the pan, lower the heat and cook for 7-10 minutes, until the skate flesh just parts from the central cartilaginous layer.
4 While the fish is cooking, put the capers into a small pan with the cream. Stir in the parsley and season with salt and pepper. Bring to the boil, lower the heat and simmer for 1 minute. Take off the heat and stir in the remaining vinegar. Check the seasoning.
5 Lift the skate from the poaching liquor onto warmed serving plates. Spoon on the cream sauce and garnish with parsley sprigs. Serve immediately.

NOTE Drain the skate scrupulously as you lift it from the poaching liquor and flick off any flavouring debris adhering to the fish.

SALMON PIE WITH PARMESAN CRUST

PREPARATION TIME 30 minutes, plus chilling
COOKING TIME About 55 minutes
FREEZING Suitable
❄

SERVES 8
- *225 g (8 oz) butter*
- *50 g (2 oz) onion, peeled and finely chopped*
- *400 g (14 oz) white plain flour*
- *450 ml (15 fl oz) fish stock*
- *150 ml (5 fl oz) dry white wine*
- *900 g (2 lb) salmon fillet, skinned and cut into chunks*

720 CALS/SERVING
- *225 g (8 oz) queen scallops (optional)*
- *125 g (4 oz) Gruyère cheese*
- *salt and pepper*
- *75 g (3 oz) freshly grated Parmesan cheese*
- *1 egg, beaten*
- *beaten egg, to glaze*
- *chopped fresh herbs, to garnish (optional)*

1 Melt 50 g (2 oz) butter in a medium saucepan. Sauté the onion, stirring, for 5-6 minutes or until softened but not coloured.
2 Off the heat, stir in 50 g (2 oz) flour, the stock and wine. Bring to the boil, stirring, then simmer for 3-4 minutes until thickened. Remove from the heat, and allow to cool slightly.
3 Add the salmon, the scallops (if using) and the Gruyère cheese. Season to taste, then turn into a 1.7 litre (3 pint) shallow, ovenproof dish and leave to cool.

4 Rub the remaining butter into the rest of the flour, then stir in the Parmesan. Add the beaten egg and 45-60 ml (3-4 tbsp) cold water. Bind the pastry together with your hands, adding extra water, if necessary.
5 Turn out onto a floured surface and knead lightly until smooth. Cover and chill for about 15 minutes.
6 Roll out the pastry and cover the filling, pressing the edges down well. Trim any excess pastry and re-roll.
7 Cut out holly leaves from the trimmings. Brush the pie with beaten egg and cover with the leaves. Brush with egg again, then chill for 15-20 minutes.
8 Bake at 190°C (375°F) mark 5 for 45-50 minutes or until crisp, covering loosely with foil if necessary. Serve immediately, sprinkling herbs over each serving, if wished.

ROAST SALMON IN MUSTARD BUTTER

PREPARATION TIME 10 minutes
COOKING TIME 20 minutes
FREEZING Not suitable
🕐

SERVES 6
- *1.1 kg (2½ lb) piece of boned middle cut of salmon*
- *175 g (6 oz) butter, melted*
- *45 ml (3 tbsp) wholegrain mustard*

560 CALS/SERVING
- *20 ml (4 tsp) dried dill*
- *salt and pepper*
- *300 g (10 oz) fresh spinach, rocket or mixed salad leaves*

1 Open out the salmon like a book until almost flat by pressing along the backbone area. Place skin-side up in a shallow ovenproof dish just large enough to hold it.
2 Mix together the butter, mustard, dill and seasoning. Pour over the salmon. Cook at 230°C (450°F) mark 8 for about 20 minutes or until just tender.
3 Toss the salad leaves and season well. Place on large plates.
4 Cut the salmon into thick slices and serve on top of the salad leaves with the mustard butter spooned over the top.

SMOKED SALMON FISHCAKES

PREPARATION TIME 45 minutes, plus chilling
COOKING TIME About 45 minutes
FREEZING Suitable (stage 4)

❊

SERVES 12

- *1.1 kg (2½ lb) old potatoes*
- *salt and pepper*
- *450 g (1 lb) salmon fillet, skinned*
- *150 ml (5 fl oz) white wine*
- *juice of 1 lemon*
- *450 g (1 lb) smoked salmon pieces*
- *10 ml (2 tsp) anchovy essence*
- *30 ml (2 tbsp) chopped fresh dill or 10 ml (2 tsp) dried dill*

380 CALS/SERVING

- *1 spring onion, finely chopped*
- *flour for coating*
- *3 eggs, beaten*
- *350 g (12 oz) fresh white breadcrumbs*
- *oil for frying*
- *lemon wedges and fresh dill, to garnish*

1 Boil the potatoes until tender, then drain, mash and season with salt and pepper. Keep warm.
2 Meanwhile, poach the salmon fillet in a covered saucepan with wine and lemon juice for about 15 minutes or until just cooked. Cool the salmon in the liquid, then coarsely flake the fish. (The liquid can be frozen for stock.)
3 Roughly chop the smoked salmon, then mix it with the fresh salmon, anchovy essence, dill and spring onion. Beat half the fish mixture into the warm potatoes. Fold in the remaining fish and season to taste. Spread the mixture on a baking sheet lined with greaseproof paper to a depth of 4 cm (1½ inches). Cover and chill for about 2 hours.
4 Shape the mixture into 24 fishcakes. Dip them in the flour, beaten egg and breadcrumbs to coat.
5 Shallow fry the fishcakes a batch at a time in 5 mm (¼ inch) of hot oil for about 4 minutes on each side or until golden and crisp. Drain on absorbent kitchen paper and keep warm while cooking the remainder. Garnish with lemon wedges and fresh dill to serve.

NOTE When coating any food in egg and breadcrumbs, it is best to have plates of flour, beaten egg and breadcrumbs lined up on the work surface. Use one hand for dipping and coating the food into the dry ingredients and the other hand for dipping into the egg.

The fishcakes can be cooked in the oven if preferred – place on a lightly greased baking sheet, brush lightly with melted butter and cook at 220°C (425°F) mark 7 for about 25 minutes.

TIPS

Smoked salmon trimmings can be bought from fishmongers more cheaply than slices. Quality varies, so check before buying.

These fishcakes freeze well, making an excellent standby for instant meals over the Christmas holiday period.

WINTER FISH STEW

PREPARATION TIME 15 minutes, plus soaking
COOKING TIME 45-50 minutes
FREEZING Not suitable

SERVES 8
- *good pinch of saffron strands*
- *about 1.8 kg (4 lb) mixed fish fillets, such as red mullet, plaice or cod, skinned*
- *90 ml (6 tbsp) olive oil*
- *2 large onions, peeled and finely chopped*
- *4 garlic cloves, peeled and crushed*
- *1 red pepper, deseeded and sliced*
- *900 g (2 lb) tomatoes, skinned, deseeded and chopped*

420 CALS/SERVING
- *4 anchovy fillets, drained*
- *300 ml (10 fl oz) dry white wine*
- *4 bay leaves*
- *90 ml (6 tbsp) chopped fresh basil*
- *salt and pepper*
- *20-24 cooked peeled prawns*
- *150 g (5 oz) cooked shelled mussels*
- *8 slices of toast*
- *chopped fresh parsley, to garnish*

1 Soak the saffron strands in a little boiling water for 30 minutes.
2 Meanwhile, cut the fish into chunky pieces.
3 Heat the oil in a saucepan, add the onions, garlic and pepper, and fry gently for 5 minutes.
4 Add the tomatoes and anchovies and stir to break them up. Add the wine and 300 ml (10 fl oz) water, bring to the boil, then lower the heat and add the bay leaves and half the basil. Simmer, uncovered, for 20 minutes.
5 Add the firm-textured fish to the tomato mixture, strain in the saffron water and season to taste. Cook for 10 minutes, then add the delicate-textured fish and cook for 5 minutes more.
6 Add the prawns and mussels, cover and cook for 3-5 minutes until warm. Remove the bay leaves and discard.
7 Put one slice of toast in each of eight soup bowls and spoon over the stew. Serve garnished with chopped parsley.

MUSSELS WITH GINGER, CHILLI AND CORIANDER

PREPARATION TIME 20 minutes
COOKING TIME 10 minutes
FREEZING Not suitable
♡ ⏱

SERVES 2

348 CALS/SERVING

- *1 kg (2¼ lb) mussels in their shells*
- *15 g (½ oz) fresh coriander sprigs*
- *1 bunch spring onions, trimmed and shredded*
- *2 garlic cloves, peeled and finely chopped*
- *2.5 cm (1 inch) piece fresh root ginger, peeled and finely chopped*
- *1 small red chilli, deseeded and cut into slivers*
- *150 ml (5 fl oz) white wine*
- *40 g (1½ oz) butter*
- *coriander sprigs, to garnish*

1 Discard any mussels with damaged shells, or any that remain open when tapped smartly on the shell. Scrub the mussels thoroughly under cold running water, pulling away the coarse threads (beards) from the side of the shells.
2 Strip the leaves from the coriander and set aside; reserve the coriander stalks.
3 Put the spring onions, garlic, ginger, chilli and coriander stalks in a saucepan which is large enough to hold the mussels. Add the wine and 150 ml (5 fl oz) water. Bring to the boil and simmer for 2 minutes.
4 Add the mussels to the pan, cover with a tight-fitting lid and cook for 4-5 minutes over a moderate heat, shaking the pan occasionally, until the shells open. Turn the mussels into a colander set over a bowl. Discard the coriander stalks and any unopened mussels.
5 Pour the liquid from the bowl back into the pan. Place over a low heat and whisk in the butter, a piece at a time, then add the coriander leaves.
6 Transfer the mussels to individual serving dishes and pour over the sauce. Serve at once, garnished with coriander sprigs.

VARIATION Replace the wine with 150 ml (5 fl oz) coconut milk for an exotic sauce.

OYSTERS AU GRATIN

PREPARATION TIME 20 minutes
COOKING TIME 10 minutes
FREEZING Not suitable
♡ ⏱

SERVES 4-6

220-150 CALS/SERVING

- *50 g (2 oz) streaky bacon, finely chopped*
- *75 g (3 oz) celery, finely chopped*
- *200 g (7 oz) can artichoke hearts, drained and finely chopped*
- *12 large oysters*
- *200 g (7 oz) mozzarella cheese, thinly sliced*

1 In a small frying pan, fry the bacon until the fat begins to run. Add the celery and artichokes. Cook, stirring, for 2 minutes. Cool.
2 Scrub the oyster shells well. Open the oysters by inserting an oyster knife into the hinge linking the shells and cutting through the muscle. Prise the shells apart and discard the flatter ones.
3 Spoon a little of the bacon and artichoke mixture over each oyster. Top with cheese.
4 Cook under a medium grill for 10 minutes.

MUSTARD-ROASTED TURKEY

PREPARATION TIME 30 minutes, plus standing
COOKING TIME 3¾-4 hours
FREEZING Not suitable

SERVES 8

650 CALS/SERVING

- *oven-ready turkey, about 4.5 kg (10 lb)*
- *45 ml (3 tbsp) wholegrain or Dijon mustard*
- *butter or margarine*
- *salt and pepper*
- *about 450 ml (15 fl oz) turkey or chicken stock*
- *60 ml (4 tbsp) sherry (optional)*
- *grated rind and juice of 1 orange*
- *cornflour*
- *fresh rosemary and sage, to garnish*

STUFFING
- *450 g (1 lb) onions, peeled and finely chopped*
- *50 g (2 oz) butter*
- *45 ml (3 tbsp) chopped fresh sage, or 10 ml (2 tsp) dried sage*
- *225 g (8 oz) fresh breadcrumbs*
- *125 g (4 oz) medium oatmeal*
- *grated rind and juice of 1 orange*
- *salt and pepper*
- *1 egg, beaten*

1 To make the stuffing, sauté the onions in the butter for 6-7 minutes or until beginning to soften. Mix with the sage and breadcrumbs.
2 Toast the oatmeal under the grill and stir into the breadcrumb mixture with the grated orange rind and 30 ml (2 tbsp) orange juice. Season well and bind with beaten egg. Cool.
3 Spoon the stuffing into the neck end of the turkey only. Shape into a neat rounded end, then tuck the neck skin under the bird and secure firmly with a small skewer or wooden cocktail stick. Place any remaining stuffing in a buttered ovenproof dish, dot with butter and cover with foil. Weigh the turkey and calculate the cooking time.
4 Place the turkey on a large, strong sheet of foil, in a large roasting tin. Spread the breast and legs thinly with the mustard. Dot the turkey generously with butter and grind over some pepper. Fold the foil around the turkey to enclose it.
5 Cook at 180°C (350°F) mark 4 for about 3 hours. Fold the foil back, baste well and return to the oven for a further 45 minutes-1 hour. Put the stuffing in the oven to bake for about 1 hour. The turkey will be a rich golden brown.
6 Lift the turkey onto a warmed serving dish, cover with foil and leave to rest for 30 minutes to make carving easier.
7 Pour the cooking liquor into a saucepan and skim. Add the stock, sherry, grated orange rind and juice. Boil for 4-5 minutes to reduce slightly.
8 Mix about 60 ml (4 tbsp) cornflour to a smooth paste with a little water. Stir into the pan juices and bring to the boil. Simmer for 1-2 minutes or until slightly thickened. Adjust the seasoning. Garnish the turkey with sprigs of fresh rosemary and sage, and serve with the gravy.

ORIENTAL TURKEY

PREPARATION TIME 20 minutes, plus standing
COOKING TIME 1 hour
FREEZING Ginger butter (stage 1)

❄

SERVES 6

765 CALS/SERVING

- *1.8 kg (4 lb) oven-ready turkey saddle or breast, bone in*
- *lychees and limes, to decorate*
- *apple and plum sauce, to serve (see Note)*
GINGER BUTTER
- *5 cm (2 inch) piece fresh root ginger, peeled and finely grated*
- *125 g (4 oz) butter, softened*

- *salt and pepper*
GLAZE
- *5 cm (2 inch) piece fresh root ginger, peeled and finely grated*
- *30 ml (2 tbsp) each light soy sauce and rice or distilled malt vinegar*
- *90 ml (6 tbsp) clear honey*
- *salt and pepper*

1 To make the ginger butter, beat the ginger with the butter and season well.
2 To make the glaze, mix all the ingedients together and season to taste.
3 Carefully loosen the turkey skin and push the soft ginger butter evenly underneath.
4 Place the turkey in a roasting tin and brush with the ginger glaze. Cover with foil and cook at 190°C (375°F) mark 5 for 15 minutes per 450 g (1 lb). Baste frequently with the glaze.
5 Uncover the turkey for the last 15 minutes to brown the skin. At this stage baste the breast again with any remaining glaze.
6 Rest the turkey for 15 minutes before carving. Serve with apple and plum sauce (see Note).

NOTE To make the accompanying apple and plum sauce, peel, core and chop 900 g (2 lb) apples and cook over a low heat with 30 ml (2 tbsp) caster sugar and 150 ml (5 fl oz) water until soft. Add the grated rind and juice of 1 lime and 50 ml (2 fl oz) oriental plum sauce. Work in a blender until smooth. Season. Reheat gently to serve hot or serve cold. Garnish with chopped chillies.

TURKEY, APRICOT AND HAZELNUT PILAFF

PREPARATION TIME 20 minutes
COOKING TIME 45 minutes
FREEZING Not suitable

SERVES 4 — 540 CALS/SERVING

- 30 ml (2 tbsp) hazelnut or olive oil
- 8 baby onions, peeled and halved
- 2 garlic cloves, peeled and crushed
- 15 ml (1 tbsp) medium curry powder
- 10 ml (2 tsp) ground coriander
- 5 ml (1 tsp) ground mixed spice
- 2 celery sticks, thickly sliced
- 125 g (4 oz) dried apricots, halved
- 225 g (8 oz) easy-cook brown rice
- 750 ml (1¼ pints) chicken stock
- 350 g (12 oz) cold cooked turkey, shredded
- 125 g (4 oz) French beans, trimmed and halved
- 50 g (2 oz) hazelnuts, toasted
- 30 ml (2 tbsp) chopped fresh parsley
- salt and pepper

1 Heat the oil in a heavy-based saucepan, add the onions, garlic, spices and celery and fry for 10 minutes until browned. Add the apricots and rice and stir-fry for 1 minute until all the grains are glossy.
2 Pour in the stock, stir well and bring to the boil. Cover and simmer gently for 20 minutes. Stir in all the remaining ingredients, and cook for a further 10 minutes. Remove from the heat and leave undisturbed for 5 minutes. Season to taste and serve at once.

VARIATION This dish can be adapted to serve cold as part of a salad spread. Chop an onion and fry in the oil with the garlic and spices for 5 minutes. Leave until cold and fold into 150 ml (5 fl oz) bought mayonnaise. In a large bowl, combine the turkey with 350 g (12 oz) cooked brown rice and the sliced raw celery, French beans, chopped dried apricots, toasted hazelnuts and parsley. Toss in the mayonnaise and serve.

ROASTED PECAN CHICKEN

PREPARATION TIME 25 minutes
COOKING TIME 1½ hours
FREEZING Not suitable

SERVES 4

430 CALS/SERVING

- *50 g (2 oz) creamy goats' cheese*
- *7.5 ml (1½ tsp) lemon juice*
- *75 g (3 oz) pecan nuts*
- *1 small garlic clove, peeled*
- *30 ml (2 tbsp) olive oil*
- *salt and pepper*

- *1.6 kg (3½ lb) oven-ready chicken*
- *lemon and onion slices*
- *150 ml (5 fl oz) dry white wine*
- *300 ml (10 fl oz) chicken stock*
- *about 10-15 ml (2-3 tsp) cornflour*

1 Place the first five ingredients in a food processor and season with black pepper only. Blend until the mixture forms a paste.
2 Loosen the skin around the chicken breast and spread the mixture underneath the skin to form an even layer. Try not to pierce or break the skin. Secure the skin with a cocktail stick and tie the chicken legs together.
3 Place the chicken in a roasting tin with the lemon and onion slices, wine and 150 ml (5 fl oz) stock. Cook at 200°C (400°F) mark 6 for about 1½ hours, basting occasionally. If necessary, cover with foil towards the end of the cooking time. Test the thickest part of the thigh with a fine skewer – when cooked, the juices run clear.
4 Keep the chicken warm. Discard the lemon and onion slices. Skim the fat from the juices and stir in the remaining 150 ml (5 fl oz) stock. Bring to the boil, scraping any sediment off the base of the pan. Mix the cornflour to a smooth paste with a little water. Off the heat, stir it into the pan juices. Return to the heat and bring to the boil, stirring all the time. Bubble for 2-3 minutes. Adjust the seasoning and serve with the chicken.

VARIATIONS Beat together 50 g (2 oz) butter with 30 ml (2 tbsp) pesto sauce. Spread this under the chicken-breast skin and over the legs and cook as above. Stir 45 ml (3 tbsp) fromage frais into the gravy just before serving.
- Beat together 45 ml (3 tbsp) olive oil with 30 ml (2 tbsp) sun-dried tomato paste. Spread underneath the chicken-breast skin. Cook as above. If

you can't find the paste, use 75 g (3 oz) sun-dried tomatoes in oil. Purée with a little olive oil.
• Beat together 50 g (2 oz) softened butter with 5 ml (1 tsp) dried tarragon and the grated rind of 1 lemon. Spread underneath the chicken-breast skin and over the legs and cook as before, using dry vermouth instead of the wine.
• Beat together 50 g (2 oz) softened butter with 5 ml (1 tsp) each of ground cumin, ground coriander and ground turmeric, 1.25 ml (¼ tsp) mild chilli powder and 1 crushed garlic clove. Spread underneath the chicken-breast skin and over the legs, and cook as before.

CHICKEN HOTPOT WITH LEEKS

PREPARATION TIME 15 minutes
COOKING TIME 1 hour 35 minutes
FREEZING Not suitable
♡

SERVES 4	350 CALS/SERVING
• *15 ml (1 tbsp) olive oil*	• *175 ml (6 fl oz) chicken stock*
• *1 large garlic clove, peeled and crushed*	• *10 ml (2 tsp) cornflour*
• *700 g (1½ lb) trimmed leeks, thickly sliced*	• *8 skinless, boneless chicken thighs, about 350 g (12 oz) total weight*
• *200 g (7 oz) reduced-fat soft cheese with garlic and herbs*	• *salt and pepper*
• *125 ml (4 fl oz) white wine*	• *300 g (10 oz) potatoes, unpeeled and thinly sliced*

1 Heat the oil in a flameproof casserole. Add the garlic and leeks and cook for about 5 minutes or until beginning to soften.
2 Meanwhile, place the cheese, wine, stock and cornflour in a food processor and blend for about 30 seconds or until smooth.
3 Arrange the chicken thighs on top of the leeks, pour the cheese mixture over and season to taste. Layer the potatoes on top of the chicken. Place a lightly oiled sheet of greaseproof paper on top of the potatoes, then cover with a lid or foil.
4 Cook at 180°C (350°F) mark 4 for 1½ hours or until the potatoes are quite tender. Brown the potatoes under a hot grill before serving.

CHICKEN IN SMOKY BACON SAUCE

PREPARATION TIME 10 minutes
COOKING TIME 20 minutes
FREEZING Not suitable
♡ ⏱

SERVES 4	350 CALS/SERVING
• *30 ml (2 tbsp) vegetable oil*	• *salt and pepper*
• *125 g (4 oz) chopped bacon pieces*	• *1 bunch spring onions, trimmed and roughly chopped*
• *4 skinless chicken breast fillets, each weighing about 150 g (5 oz)*	• *225 g (8 oz) crisp red apples, thickly sliced*
• *200 ml (7 fl oz) apple juice*	• *60 ml (4 tbsp) crème fraîche*
• *15 ml (1 tbsp) chopped fresh thyme or 5 ml (1 tsp) dried thyme*	

1 Heat the oil in a large deep frying pan or sauté pan. Add the chopped bacon and chicken pieces and fry for a few minutes until golden, stirring and turning occasionally.
2 Stir in the apple juice and thyme, and season to taste. Bring to the boil, cover and simmer for 10 minutes.
3 Uncover, then add the spring onions. Tip the apples into the pan and cook over a high heat for about 5 minutes or until the liquid has reduced by half and the chicken is tender.
4 Reduce the heat to low and stir in the crème fraîche. Adjust the seasoning and serve.

NOTE Chopped bacon pieces are sold in most supermarkets, but if unavailable, simply buy thin-cut, smoked, streaky bacon and chop roughly yourself.

SWEET GINGERED CHICKEN

PREPARATION TIME 10 minutes
COOKING TIME About 30 minutes
FREEZING Not suitable

SERVES 6
- *120 ml (8 tbsp) apricot jam*
- *75 ml (5 tbsp) light soy sauce*
- *120 ml (8 tbsp) dry sherry*
- *juice of 1 lemon*
- *2 garlic cloves, peeled and crushed*
- *2.5 cm (1 inch) piece fresh root ginger, peeled and finely grated*

435 CALS/SERVING
- *350 g (12 oz) aubergine, thinly sliced*
- *6 chicken breast fillets with skin, each weighing about 150 g (5 oz)*

1 Mix together the first four ingredients. Add the garlic and the ginger.
2 Line a large roasting tin with foil. Spread out the aubergine and chicken in the tin. Spoon the ginger mixture over the top.
3 Cook at 220°C (425°F) mark 7 for about 30-35 minutes, basting occasionally, until the chicken and aubergine are well browned and glazed. Add a little water, if necessary, towards the end of cooking.

WINTER CHICKEN

PREPARATION TIME 20 minutes
COOKING TIME 45 minutes
FREEZING Not suitable
♡

SERVES 4
- *4 chicken leg portions, about 700 g (1½ lb) total weight*
- *salt and pepper*
- *15 ml (1 tbsp) white plain flour*
- *15 ml (1 tbsp) olive oil*
- *225 g (8 oz) onion, peeled and cut into small wedges*
- *450 g (1 lb) carrots, peeled and cut into chunks*
- *450 g (1 lb) celery, cut into chunks*

350 CALS/SERVING
- *50 g (2 oz) rindless lean back bacon, roughly chopped*
- *200 ml (7 fl oz) apple juice*
- *400 g (14 oz) can butter beans (300 g/10 oz drained weight)*
- *1 bunch watercress, roughly chopped*
- *15-30 ml (1-2 tbsp) lemon juice*

1 Skin the chicken portions and divide them into thighs and drumsticks. Toss the chicken in seasoned flour.
2 Heat the oil in a medium-size, flameproof casserole. Add the onion, carrots, celery and bacon and fry for 2-3 minutes. Mix in the apple juice, drained butter beans and the chicken.
3 Bring to the boil on the hob, cover and cook in the oven at 180°C (350°F) mark 4 for about 45 minutes or until all the ingredients are tender.
4 Stir the watercress into the casserole with the lemon juice and seasoning to taste before serving.

MARINATED CHICKEN WITH PRUNES

PREPARATION TIME 10 minutes, plus marinating
COOKING TIME 50 minutes
FREEZING Not suitable

SERVES 4

- *4 chicken quarters (breast or leg), about 900 g (2 lb) total weight*
- *4 garlic cloves, peeled and sliced*
- *10 ml (2 tsp) dried mixed herbs*
- *30 ml (2 tbsp) red wine vinegar*
- *125 ml (4 fl oz) vegetable oil*
- *225 g (8 oz) pitted no-soak prunes*
- *30 ml (2 tbsp) capers, drained*

570 CALS/SERVING

- *salt and pepper*
- *300 ml (10 fl oz) dry white wine*
- *25 g (1 oz) demerara sugar*
- *5 ml (1 tsp) cornflour*
- *150 ml (5 fl oz) chicken stock*
- *about 5 ml (1 tsp) lemon juice*
- *flat-leaf parsley, to garnish*

1 Place the chicken in a large non-metallic bowl with the garlic. Add the next five ingredients with plenty of seasoning and mix well. Cover and marinate in the refrigerator overnight.

2 Remove the chicken from the marinade and reserve the marinade. With a little oil from the marinade, brown the chicken in a flameproof casserole large enough to hold the chicken in a single layer. Pour the remaining marinade, with the prunes and capers, over the chicken. Pour over the wine and sprinkle with the sugar. Bring to the boil.

3 Cover and bake at 180°C (350°F) mark 4 for 30 minutes, then uncover and baste. Return to the oven, uncovered, for a further 20 minutes, or until the chicken quarters are cooked through.

4 Using slotted spoons, lift the chicken into a serving dish. Cover the chicken and keep it warm. Skim the juices. Mix the cornflour to a smooth paste with 15 ml (1 tbsp) water. Add to the pan juices with the stock and bring to the boil, stirring all the time. Cook for 1-2 minutes. Adjust the seasoning, add about 5 ml (1 tsp) lemon juice to taste, spoon over the chicken and serve, garnished with flat-leaf parsley.

GOOSE WITH PRUNE STUFFING

PREPARATION TIME 30 minutes
COOKING TIME 1¾-2¼ hours
FREEZING Not suitable

SERVES 10

- *4-5 kg (9-11 lb) oven-ready goose, with giblets*
- *salt and pepper*
- *450 g (1 lb) prunes, soaked overnight*
- *300 ml (10 fl oz) dry white wine*
- *50 g (2 oz) butter*
- *1 small onion, peeled and finely chopped*

480-600 CALS/SERVING

- *30 ml (2 tbsp) port*
- *125 g (4 oz) fresh breadcrumbs*
- *5 ml (1 tsp) white plain flour*
- *caramelized clementines and roasted onion wedges, to garnish*

1 Pull the inside fat out of the goose and reserve. Prick the skin of the goose with a fork in several places. Rub salt over the skin.
2 Drain the prunes and put in a saucepan with the wine. Bring to the boil and simmer for about 10 minutes or until tender. Remove the prunes from the liquid, discard the stones, chop the flesh and put in a bowl. Reserve the cooking liquid.
3 Melt 40 g (1½ oz) of the butter in another pan, add the onion and cook gently until soft but not coloured. Separate the goose liver from the giblets and chop finely. Add to the onion and cook gently for 2-3 minutes, then mix with the prunes.

4 Add the port to the pan and bubble for 1 minute, scraping the pan to dislodge any sediment. Pour the liquid into the prune mixture, add the breadcrumbs and mix well. Allow to cool for 10 minutes.
5 Spoon the stuffing into the neck cavity of the goose. Skewer the neck skin to the back of the bird, then truss and tie up the goose with string. Weigh the bird and calculate the cooking time, allowing 15 minutes per 450 g (1 lb) plus 15 minutes.
6 Put the goose on a wire rack in a roasting tin. Cover the breast with the reserved fat and foil. Roast in the oven at 200°C (400°F) mark 6, basting frequently. Remove the foil for the last 30 minutes to brown.
7 When the goose is cooked, transfer to a serving dish and keep warm in a low oven. Pour off all but 30 ml (2 tbsp) fat from the juices in the roasting tin. Transfer to the top of the cooker and blend in the flour. Cook for 1 minute until just colouring, then slowly add the reserved prune liquid, stirring well. Bring to the boil and simmer for 2-3 minutes. Season to taste and whisk in the remaining butter. Serve the sauce with the garnished goose.

NOTE For the clementine garnish, make a butter and brown sugar syrup, add the peeled fruit and coat well.

DUCKLING BREASTS WITH ARMAGNAC

PREPARATION TIME 5 minutes, plus marinating
COOKING TIME 25 minutes
FREEZING Not suitable
♡

SERVES 6

240 CALS/SERVING

- 6 duckling breast fillets, each weighing about 175 g (6 oz)
- salt and pepper
- 2 shallots or small onions, peeled and finely chopped
- 2 garlic cloves, peeled and crushed
- 75 ml (5 tbsp) Armagnac
- sprigs of fresh thyme
- bay leaves
- sprigs of fresh herbs, to garnish

1 Score the duckling skin and rub with salt. Place the breasts side by side in a shallow non-metallic dish.
2 Mix the shallots or onions with the garlic and Armagnac and spoon over the duckling breasts. Add sprigs of fresh thyme, bay leaves and plenty of black pepper. Turn the duckling in the marinade, cover and marinate at room temperature for about 1 hour.
3 Place the duckling breasts on a wire rack standing over a roasting tin. Baste with marinade.
4 Roast at 230°C (450°F) mark 8 for 10 minutes, then lower the temperature to 200°C (400°F) mark 6 for a further 10-15 minutes.
5 Serve thickly sliced, garnished with sprigs of fresh herbs.

ROAST DUCKLING WITH SHERRY VINEGAR

PREPARATION TIME 15 minutes
COOKING TIME 50 minutes
FREEZING Not suitable

SERVES 6

390 CALS/SERVING

- salt and pepper
- 6 duckling breast fillets, each weighing about 175 g (6 oz)
- 125 g (4 oz) sugar
- 60 ml (4 tbsp) each dry sherry and white wine vinegar or 120 ml (8 tbsp) sherry vinegar
- 900 ml (1½ pints) chicken stock
- 350 g (12 oz) carrots, peeled and roughly chopped
- 225 g (8 oz) turnips, peeled and roughly chopped
- 40 g (1½ oz) butter
- 125 g (4 oz) spring onions, trimmed and roughly chopped
- 125 g (4 oz) mangetout, trimmed
- lemon juice

1 Season the duckling breast fillets and place in a roasting tin. Cook at 230°C (450°F) mark 8 for 10 minutes, then reduce the temperature to 200°C (400°F) mark 6 for about a further 20 minutes.
2 Meanwhile, place the sugar, the dry sherry and white wine vinegar in a heavy-based pan and cook over a gentle heat until the sugar dissolves and caramelizes to a deep golden colour. Add the chicken stock and bring to the boil, stirring. Boil to reduce by half, then set aside.
3 Place the carrots and turnips in a saucepan with 150 ml (5 fl oz) water, 25 g (1 oz) butter and a pinch each of salt, pepper and sugar. Bring to the boil, then cover and simmer for about 15 minutes until the vegetables are just tender and the liquid has evaporated to leave the vegetables glazed and shiny. Boil off excess liquid if necessary.
4 Blanch the spring onions and mangetout in boiling salted water for 1-2 minutes. Drain.
5 To finish, leave the duckling to rest in a warm place for about 10 minutes, then carve into thick slices. Bring the sauce to a simmer, whisk in the remaining butter and sharpen with lemon juice. Adjust the seasoning.
6 Reheat the vegetables in the sauce. Arrange the duckling and vegetables on a large serving platter and serve.

CRISPY CHINESE DUCK WITH ORIENTAL VEGETABLES

PREPARATION TIME 10 minutes
COOKING TIME 20 minutes
FREEZING Not suitable
🕐

SERVES 6

- *6 duckling breasts, each weighing about 175 g (6 oz)*
- *salt and pepper*
- *45 ml (3 tbsp) vegetable oil*
- *30 ml (2 tbsp) sesame oil*
- *90 ml (6 tbsp) yellow bean sauce*
- *45 ml (3 tbsp) caster sugar*
- *2 garlic cloves, peeled and crushed*
- *1 cm (¹/₂ inch) piece fresh root ginger, peeled and finely chopped*
- *15 ml (1 tbsp) sesame seeds*

410 CALS/SERVING

- *125 g (4 oz) cabbage, cut into fine strips*
- *125 g (4 oz) carrots, peeled and cut into fine strips*
- *1 red pepper, deseeded and cut into fine strips*
- *75 g (3 oz) baby corn, quartered*
- *5 cm (2 inch) piece cucumber, cut into fine strips*
- *6 spring onions, cut into fine strips*

1 Prick the skin of the duck breasts well with a fork and rub with salt and pepper. Place on a baking sheet on the top shelf of the oven and cook at 230°C (450°F) mark 8 for about 15-20 minutes or until the duck is just cooked, but still pink.
2 Meanwhile, heat 15 ml (1 tbsp) of each oil in a frying pan, add the yellow bean sauce, sugar and 30 ml (2 tbsp) water, and cook for 1 minute. Remove and leave to cool.
3 Heat both remaining oils in the rinsed and dried frying pan. Add the garlic, ginger and sesame seeds and stir for about 1 minute or until golden brown. Add the cabbage, carrots, pepper and baby corn and stir-fry briskly for 2-3 minutes. Remove from the heat and stir in the cucumber and spring onions.
4 Carve the duck into slices and arrange on top of the vegetables. Serve immediately with the sauce.

VARIATION Use chicken breast pieces instead of duckling.

CHRISTMAS PHEASANT

PREPARATION TIME 30 minutes
COOKING TIME 2¼ hours
FREEZING Suitable (stage 4)
❄

SERVES 6

- *2 oven-ready pheasants*
- *salt and pepper*
- *30 ml (2 tbsp) vegetable oil*
- *50 g (2 oz) butter*
- *225 g (8 oz) shallots or small onions, peeled*
- *225 g (8 oz) streaky bacon, chopped*
- *2 garlic cloves, peeled and crushed*
- *300 ml (10 fl oz) Madeira*
- *600 ml (1 pint) beef stock*

490 CALS/SERVING

- *sprig of fresh thyme or pinch of dried*
- *2 bay leaves*
- *6 juniper berries*
- *pared rind and juice of 1 orange*
- *90 ml (6 tbsp) redcurrant jelly*
- *225 g (8 oz) fresh cranberries*
- *225 g (8 oz) cooked chestnuts*
- *fresh thyme, to garnish*

1 Joint both pheasants into four, discarding backbone and knuckles. Season to taste.
2 Heat the oil and butter in a large, flameproof casserole and brown the shallots and bacon. Remove and set aside. Add the pheasant, half at a time, and fry for 5-6 minutes or until golden. Remove the pheasant from the casserole.
3 Stir in the garlic, half the Madeira, the stock, thyme, bay leaves, juniper berries and pared orange rind. Bring to the boil and add the pheasant. Cover and cook at 170°C (325°F) mark 3 for 1 hour.
4 Add the shallots, bacon and redcurrant jelly. Re-cover and return to the oven for 45 minutes or until the pheasant is quite tender.
5 Meanwhile, marinate the cranberries and chestnuts in the remaining Madeira and the orange juice for 30 minutes.
6 Remove the pheasant, vegetables and bacon from the liquid, cover and keep warm. Bubble the sauce for about 5 minutes to reduce to a syrupy consistency. Add the cranberry and chestnut mixture and simmer for a further 5 minutes. Adjust the seasoning and spoon the sauce over the pheasant. Serve garnished with fresh thyme.

QUAILS ON GNOCCHI WITH CREAM SAUCE

PREPARATION TIME 25 minutes, plus cooling
COOKING TIME About 1 hour
FREEZING Not suitable

SERVES 6

- 6 oven-ready quails
- salt and pepper
- 6 thin rashers pancetta or smoked streaky bacon
- 25 g (1 oz) butter
- 50 g (2 oz) pine nuts
- 75 ml (5 tbsp) white wine
- 25 g (1 oz) raisins
- 75 ml (5 tbsp) double cream
- 15 ml (1 tbsp) chopped fresh tarragon
- sprigs of tarragon and parsley, to garnish

550 CALS/SERVING
GNOCCHI

- 450 g (1 lb) floury potatoes, peeled and cut into small chunks
- salt
- 25 g (1 oz) butter
- 1 egg yolk
- 125 g (4 oz) white plain flour
- 15 ml (1 tbsp) chopped fresh tarragon or 5 ml (1 tsp) dried
- 15 ml (1 tbsp) chopped fresh parsley

1 To make the gnocchi, cook the potatoes in boiling salted water for 15 minutes until tender. Drain and leave to cool slightly.

2 Beat in the butter and egg yolk. Add the flour and herbs and stir until the mixture forms a firm dough. Turn out onto a lightly floured surface and divide into six portions. Shape each into a flat cake, about 1 cm (½ inch) thick.

3 Bring a saucepan of water to the boil. Add 3 of the gnocchi cakes and simmer gently for 2-3 minutes or until they rise to the surface. Turn the gnocchi and cook for a further 2 minutes. Remove with a slotted spoon and place in a lightly greased dish. Cook the remainder in the same way.

4 Season the quails and wrap a piece of bacon around each, tucking the ends underneath. Place in a small roasting tin and dot with half the butter.

5 Bake the quails at 190°C (375°F) mark 5 for 25 minutes until turning golden. Remove from the oven and place a quail on each piece of gnocchi. Return to the oven while making the sauce.

6 To make the sauce, melt the remaining butter in the roasting tin and add the pine nuts. Fry for 2-3 minutes until coloured, then add the wine. Cook briskly for 2 minutes. Lower the heat, add the raisins and cream, and cook gently to combine, adding a little water if too thick. Season and stir in the tarragon.

7 To serve, transfer the quails to warmed serving plates, spoon the sauce over and garnish.

SPICED RIB OF BEEF

PREPARATION TIME 15 minutes, plus resting
COOKING TIME 2 hours
FREEZING Not suitable

SERVES 6

- *2.3 kg (5 lb) rib of beef or 1.8 kg (4 lb) boned and rolled rib of beef*
- *75 g (3 oz) softened butter*
- *salt and pepper*
- *30 ml (2 tbsp) soft brown sugar*
- *5 ml (1 tsp) ground allspice*
- *2.5 ml (½ tsp) each ground mace and ground cloves*

725 CALS/SERVING

- *30 ml (2 tbsp) wholegrain mustard*
- *45 ml (3 tbsp) chopped fresh parsley*
- *2 garlic cloves, peeled and crushed*

GRAVY

- *45 ml (3 tbsp) white plain flour*
- *750 ml (1½ pints) beef stock or vegetable water*

1 Wipe the rib of beef and place fat side up in a roasting tin that is just large enough to hold it. Spread 25 g (1 oz) butter over the surface of the beef and season well.

2 Roast at 230°C (450°F) mark 8 for 30 minutes, then baste well. Lower the oven to 200°C (400°F) mark 6 and return the meat for a further 1 hour, basting the beef occasionally.

3 Mix together the remaining 50 g (2 oz) butter with the sugar, spices, mustard, parsley, garlic and plenty of seasoning.

4 Remove most of the fat from the roasting tin. Spread the spiced mixture evenly over the meat fat and return to the oven for a further 30 minutes, basting occasionally. Cover loosely with foil if the meat begins to overbrown.

5 Place the meat on a carving dish, loosely cover with foil and leave to rest for 15 minutes.

6 Meanwhile, prepare the gravy. Skim off the excess fat to leave 60 ml (4 tbsp) in the tin. Sprinkle in the flour and whisk over a low heat until the mixture begins to brown and is a smooth paste.

7 Gradually whisk in the stock, scraping all the sediment off the bottom of the pan. Bring to the boil, then simmer gently for 2-3 minutes, adjust the seasoning and serve with the beef.

BEEF MEDALLIONS WITH STILTON MOUSSE

PREPARATION TIME 15 minutes
COOKING TIME 15 minutes
FREEZING Not suitable

SERVES 6

- *225 g (8 oz) skinless chicken breast fillets, chilled*
- *300 ml (10 fl oz) double cream, chilled*
- *225 g (8 oz) crumbled Stilton cheese*
- *salt and pepper*
- *25 g (1 oz) butter*
- *300 g (10 oz) celery, cut into matchsticks*

630 CALS/SERVING

- *six 150 g (5 oz) fillet steaks*
- *15 ml (1 tbsp) chopped fresh parsley*
- *squeeze of lemon juice*
- *extra Stilton, to crumble (optional)*

1 Blend the chicken in a food processor until smooth. Add the cream and pulse for 2-3 seconds or until the cream is just combined. Add the Stilton cheese to the chicken in the same way. Season and refrigerate for 10 minutes.
2 Meanwhile, melt the butter in a medium saucepan, add the celery and cook gently, covered, for about 5 minutes or until just tender. Keep warm.
3 Heat a non-stick frying pan. Fry the steaks on both sides for about 3 minutes for rare (5 minutes for medium; 6-7 minutes for well done). Be careful to time your steaks accurately. Place on a hot baking sheet.
4 Divide the chilled Stilton mixture among the medallions and spread evenly over the top of each one. Grill for about 6 minutes or until the mousse turns golden brown and is firm and cooked through.
5 Add the chopped parsley and lemon juice to the celery and serve alongside the beef medallions. Crumble a little extra Stilton over the steaks, if wished.

FESTIVE BEEF CASSEROLE

PREPARATION TIME 30 minutes, plus soaking
COOKING TIME 2 hours 25 minutes
FREEZING Suitable (stage 3)
♡ ❄

SERVES 8

- *150 g (5 oz) each no-soak pitted prunes and apricots*
- *125 g (4 oz) raisins*
- *finely grated rind and juice of 1 orange*
- *200 ml (7 fl oz) orange juice*
- *150 ml (5 fl oz) dry sherry*
- *450 g (1 lb) stewing beef, cut into 4 cm (1½ inch) cubes*
- *450 g (1 lb) venison, cut into 4 cm (1½ inch) cubes*
- *5 ml (1 tsp) salt*
- *30 ml (2 tbsp) vegetable oil*

275 CALS/SERVING

- *450 g (1 lb) onions, peeled and finely sliced*
- *2.5 ml (½ tsp) each ground mace and ground cinnamon*
- *5 ml (1 tsp) black peppercorns, crushed*
- *pinch of allspice*
- *10 ml (2 tsp) coriander seeds, crushed*
- *15 ml (1 tbsp) white plain flour*
- *450 ml (15 fl oz) beef stock*
- *30 ml (2 tbsp) balsamic vinegar*

1 Soak the dried fruit in the combined orange juices and the sherry. Cover and leave for 1 hour or overnight. Season the meat with salt.
2 Heat the oil in a large, flameproof casserole and brown the meat in small batches. Ensure it is well browned so that the casserole juices will have a rich, dark colour. Add a little more oil if necessary and fry the onions until they are golden. Return all the meat to the pan with the spices, orange rind and flour. Cook, stirring, for 3 minutes. Add the beef stock and bring to the boil. Add the vinegar. Cover and cook at 150°C (300°F) mark 2 for 1 hour.
3 Remove the casserole from the oven. Strain the fruit and reserve. Add the soaking liquid to the casserole, re-cover and cook for a further 1 hour 10 minutes or until the meat is very tender. Stir in the reserved fruits and return to the oven for 5 minutes to heat through before serving.

1 Place the diced lamb in a bowl, add the next 5 ingredients and stir well. Pour the orange juice and 45 ml (3 tbsp) olive oil over. Stir. Cover the bowl and leave the lamb to marinate in the refrigerator for 3-8 hours.

2 Mix the dried apricots and raisins with the saffron, sherry and vinegar. Cover and leave to marinate at room temperature for at least 3 hours or overnight, stirring the mixture occasionally.

3 Heat the remaining olive oil in a large, flameproof casserole. Lift the meat from the marinade and brown in batches on a high heat. Lower the heat and return all the meat to the casserole dish. Add the flour and stir well. Add the marinade, soaked fruit and its liquid and lamb stock. Season, stir well and bring to the boil.

4 Cover the casserole with a tight-fitting lid and cook at 180°C (350°F) mark 4 for about 1¼ hours or until the meat is very tender. Serve the lamb with saffron rice.

FRUITY LAMB CASSEROLE WITH SPICES

PREPARATION TIME 30 minutes, plus marinating
COOKING TIME 1½ hours
FREEZING Suitable (stage 4)
❄

SERVES 8

540 CALS/SERVING

- 1.4 kg (3 lb) diced shoulder of lamb
- 10 ml (2 tsp) ground cumin
- 2.5 ml (½ tsp) ground cloves
- 10 ml (2 tsp) dried coriander
- 10 ml (2 tsp) dried thyme
- 4 garlic cloves, peeled and crushed
- 175 ml (6 fl oz) fresh orange juice
- 60 ml (4 tbsp) olive oil
- 175 g (6 oz) no-soak dried apricots

- 75 g (3 oz) raisins
- 5 ml (1 tsp) saffron strands
- 300 ml (10 fl oz) sherry
- 75 ml (3 fl oz) vinegar, preferably sherry vinegar
- 60 ml (4 tbsp) white plain flour
- 600 ml (1 pint) stock, preferably lamb stock
- salt and pepper
- saffron rice, to serve

HONEYED LEG OF LAMB WITH WINTER VEGETABLES

PREPARATION TIME 20 minutes
COOKING TIME 1½ hours
FREEZING Not suitable

SERVES 4

600 CALS/SERVING

- 1 orange
- four 10 cm (4 inch) sprigs rosemary
- 1 small half leg of lamb, weighing about 1.1 kg (2½ lb)
- 30-60 ml (2-4 tbsp) vegetable oil
- 225 g (8 oz) carrots, peeled and cut into large chunks
- 225 g (8 oz) parsnips, peeled and cut into large chunks

- 450 g (1 lb) potatoes, peeled and cut into large chunks
- 75 g (3 oz) turnip, peeled and cut into large chunks
- 6 shallots, peeled
- 300 ml (10 fl oz) white wine
- 15 ml (1 tbsp) honey
- salt and pepper

1 Pare the rind from half the orange and cut into strips about 5 mm (¼ inch) wide and 2.5 cm (1 inch) long. Squeeze the juice from the orange and reserve. Divide the rosemary into 2.5 cm (1 inch) pieces.

2 Place the lamb and 30 ml (2 tbsp) oil in a large roasting tin and, over a high heat, brown the lamb

all over. Remove from the tin using slotted spoons. Add the vegetables to the pan, adding more oil if necessary, and sauté for 4-5 minutes or until golden, stirring occasionally.

3 Meanwhile, make 10-12 incisions in the lamb and insert a piece of rosemary and orange rind in each.

4 Sprinkle the extra pieces of orange rind and rosemary over the vegetables. Top with the lamb. Mix together the white wine, juice of the orange, the honey and seasoning. Pour over the lamb.

5 Roast at 200°C (400°F) mark 6 for about 1¼ hours; for well done meat, roast for about 30 minutes longer. Serve the lamb accompanied by the vegetables with any juices spooned over.

LAMB AND LENTIL BAKE

PREPARATION TIME 20 minutes, plus cooling
COOKING TIME 1¼ hours
FREEZING Suitable (stage 4)

❄

SERVES 4

- *30 ml (2 tbsp) vegetable oil*
- *125 g (4 oz) onion, peeled and finely chopped*
- *2.5 cm (1 inch) piece fresh root ginger, peeled and finely chopped*
- *1 garlic clove, peeled and crushed*
- *2.5 ml (½ tsp) chilli seasoning*
- *2.5 ml (½ tsp) paprika*
- *2.5 ml (½ tsp) dried marjoram*

520 CALS/SERVING

- *225 g (8 oz) minced lamb*
- *175 g (6 oz) red lentils*
- *30 ml (2 tbsp) tomato purée*
- *30 ml (2 tbsp) lemon juice*
- *50 g (2 oz) raisins*
- *600 ml (1 pint) chicken stock*
- *salt and pepper*
- *50 g (2 oz) butter*
- *about 125 g (4 oz) filo pastry*
- *poppy seeds*

1 Heat the oil in a saucepan. Fry the onions until translucent, about 4-5 minutes. Stir in the ginger, garlic, chilli seasoning, paprika and marjoram. Cook, stirring, for 1 minute. Add the mince and stir until it changes colour and is free of lumps.

2 Mix in the lentils, tomato purée, lemon juice, raisins and stock. Cover and cook over a low heat for 20-25 minutes or until the lentils and mince are tender and most of the liquid is absorbed. Uncover and bubble off any excess liquid, stirring

occasionally. Adjust the seasoning then turn into a bowl and allow to cool completely.

3 Melt the butter and lightly grease a 23 cm (9 inch) base measurement, 3 cm (1¼ inch) deep, loose-based fluted flan tin. Line with sheets of filo pastry, brushing with butter between the layers and overlapping them in a random manner. There should be no gaps in the pastry and the excess pastry should hang over the sides of the tin.

4 Spoon the cold filling into the flan case. Wrap over the pastry to enclose the filling. Brush with butter and garnish with crumpled up pastry trimmings. Brush with butter again, and sprinkle with poppy seeds.

5 Cook at 190°C (375°F) mark 5 for about 50-55 minutes, covering lightly with foil after about 30-35 minutes. Cool for 10 minutes before serving.

TIP

Filo pastry sheets come in all sizes. You'll need about 125 g (4 oz) pastry sheets to line and cover the flan. Cut or trim the sheets as required so that they easily fit into the tin; use a little extra pastry if necessary. Whilst lining the tin, always keep the pastry covered with clingfilm or a tea towel as once it's exposed to air it quickly dries and becomes impossible to handle as it often breaks into pieces.

BRAISED HAM WITH MADEIRA

PREPARATION TIME 30 minutes, plus soaking
COOKING TIME 3¼-3½ hours
FREEZING Suitable: Sauce only

✳

SERVES 12-16

- *2.7 kg (6 lb) piece of gammon*
- *½ bottle medium white wine*
- *6 cloves*
- *8 peppercorns*
- *½ bottle Madeira*

SAUCE
- *300 ml (10 fl oz) dry white wine*
- *about 300 ml (10 fl oz) chicken or vegetable stock*
- *75 g (3 oz) butter*
- *40 g (1½ oz) white plain flour*

625-515 CALS/SERVING

- *6 juniper berries, crushed*
- *8 shallots, peeled and chopped*
- *6 dried green peppercorns, crushed*
- *125 ml (4 fl oz) white wine vinegar*
- *30 ml (2 tbsp) Dijon mustard*
- *125 ml (4 fl oz) crème fraîche or soured cream*
- *salt and pepper*

1 Cover the gammon with cold water and leave to soak overnight. Scrub the skin and drain and dry well. Calculate the poaching time, allowing 25 minutes per 450 g (1 lb).

2 Place the gammon in a large saucepan and cover with cold water. Bring slowly to the boil, then drain. Pour the wine into the pan and add the cloves and peppercorns and enough hot water to cover. Cover and simmer very gently for the calculated time. Allow the gammon to cool in the liquid, then drain.

3 Strip the rind off the gammon and score the fat into a diamond pattern. Place the gammon in a roasting tin and pour over the Madeira. Braise in the oven at 180°C (350°F) mark 4 for 45 minutes to 1 hour, basting frequently until golden brown, then transfer to a platter, cover loosely and keep warm while making the sauce.

4 Pour off the juices from the roasting tin into a large measuring jug and set aside. When the fat has risen to the surface, carefully skim off and reserve 30 ml (2 tbsp). Make the braising liquid up to 1.1 litres (2 pints) with the wine and stock.

5 Melt the butter and reserved ham fat in a saucepan. Add the flour and cook, stirring, for 3-4 minutes until foaming. Whisk in the wine and stock mixture. Add the juniper berries and half the

SAUTEED LIVER WITH ORANGE AND SAGE

PREPARATION TIME 10 minutes
COOKING TIME 10-15 minutes
FREEZING Not suitable

♡ ⏱

SERVES 4

- *450 g (1 lb) lamb's liver, cut into 5 cm (2 inch) strips*
- *25 g (1 oz) seasoned flour*
- *10 ml (2 tsp) chopped fresh sage or 5 ml (1 tsp) dried*

310 CALS/SERVING

- *3 large oranges*
- *15 ml (1 tbsp) vegetable oil*
- *225 g (8 oz) onion, peeled and roughly chopped*
- *chopped fresh sage or parsley, to garnish*

1 Toss the liver in the seasoned flour and sage mixed together. Using a serrated knife, peel, halve and thickly slice one orange.

2 Heat the oil in a frying pan, add the onion and cook, stirring, for about 3-4 minutes. Add the liver and toss over a high heat for a further 5-7 minutes until browned and just cooked.

3 Reduce the heat, stir in the grated rind and juice of the remaining 2 oranges and allow to heat through. Garnish with the orange slices and herbs.

shallots. Bring to the boil and simmer for 10
minutes, stirring constantly.

6 Meanwhile, put the green peppercorns,
remaining shallots and vinegar in a saucepan and
reduce to 10 ml (2 tsp). Dip the base of the pan
into cold water to stop the reduction. Stir the
Madeira sauce into the reduced vinegar with the
mustard and simmer for at least 15 minutes. Stir
in the crème fraîche or cream and bring to the
boil. Check the seasoning. Pour into a warmed
sauceboat.

7 Slice the ham and serve with the sauce and
seasonal vegetables.

HERBY RACK OF PORK WITH
ROAST VEGETABLES

PREPARATION TIME 15 minutes, plus marinating
COOKING TIME 1 hour 40 minutes
FREEZING Not suitable

SERVES 6

- *10 ml (2 tsp) each finely chopped fresh sage, oregano and rosemary or 5 ml (1 tsp) each dried*
- *15 ml (1 tbsp) chopped fresh parsley*
- *1.4 kg (3 lb) rack of pork, chined*
- *5 ml (1 tsp) each salt and coarse ground black pepper*
- *1.1 kg (2½ lb) mixed vegetables, cut into large chunks*

645 CALS/SERVING

- *275 g (10 oz) sweet potatoes or baking potatoes, cut into large chunks*
- *200 ml (7 fl oz) olive oil*
- *45 ml (3 tbsp) redcurrant jelly*
- *juice of 1 small lemon*
- *2 garlic cloves, peeled and crushed*

1 Mix all of the herbs together. Score the fat of
the pork in narrow vertical lines with a sharp
knife. Rub the joint with 30 ml (2 tbsp) herbs and
half the salt and pepper. Cover and refrigerate for
at least 1 hour or overnight.

2 Toss the vegetables and potatoes with the
remaining seasoning and 50 ml (2 fl oz) olive oil.

3 Place the vegetables in a large roasting tin, lay a
wire rack over the top and place the pork on it.
Cook at 220°C (425°F) mark 7 for 1 hour 25
minutes, turning the vegetables frequently.

4 Heat the redcurrant jelly with 30 ml (2 tbsp)
water. Bring to the boil then take off the heat.

Remove the pork from the oven and brush the
redcurrant glaze over the rind of the pork. Cook
the pork for a further 15 minutes.

5 To serve, carve the rack into chops. Toss the
vegetables with the lemon juice, garlic, the
remaining olive oil and herbs. Serve immediately
with the pork.

> **TIP**
> If the rack of pork is quite a loose shape, tie
> securely at intervals with fine string.

buttered 2 litre (3½ pint) ovenproof dish. Cover with half of the bread and sprinkle over two-thirds of the Gruyère. Add the remaining spinach, then top with the remaining bread. Pour over the egg and milk mixture. Press the bread gently into the milk.

4 Sprinkle over the remaining Gruyère and Parmesan and allow to stand for at least 30 minutes to absorb most of the liquid.

5 Place the dish in a roasting tin and pour in enough boiling water to come halfway up the sides of the dish. Bake at 220°C (425°F) mark 7 for about 30 minutes or until puffed, lightly set and well browned, covering loosely with foil if necessary.

STILTON, WALNUT AND BACON FLAN

PREPARATION TIME 10 minutes, plus pastry and chilling
COOKING TIME 50 minutes
FREEZING Suitable

❄

SERVES 4-6

- *Walnut Shortcrust Pastry, made with 175 g (6 oz) white plain flour (see page 75)*

FILLING
- *125 g (4 oz) rindless back bacon, diced*
- *10 ml (2 tsp) olive oil*

610-405 CALS/SERVING

- *2 sticks of celery, chopped*
- *75 g (3 oz) Stilton cheese, crumbled*
- *1 egg*
- *1 egg yolk*
- *150 ml (5 fl oz) single cream*
- *salt and pepper*

1 Roll out the pastry on a lightly floured surface and use to line a 20 cm (8 inch) flan tin. Prick the bottom with a fork and chill for 20 minutes.

2 Bake the flan blind (see page 75) at 200°C (400°F) mark 6 until pale golden.

3 Dry fry the bacon for 5 minutes to release the fat. Add the oil to the pan with the celery and fry for 2 minutes. Scatter the bacon, celery and Stilton over the base of the flan.

4 Beat the egg and egg yolk into the cream, and season with salt and pepper. Pour the cream mixture into the pastry case, and bake the flan for 30 minutes, until just set and golden. Serve warm or cold.

GOLDEN CHEESE AND SPINACH PUDDING

PREPARATION TIME 20 minutes, plus standing
COOKING TIME 35 minutes
FREEZING Not suitable

SERVES 4

- *450 g (1 lb) spinach leaves*
- *600 ml (1 pint) milk*
- *3 eggs*
- *60 ml (4 tbsp) freshly grated Parmesan cheese*
- *2.5 ml (½ tsp) chilli seasoning (not powder)*

625 CALS/SERVING

- *freshly grated nutmeg*
- *salt and pepper*
- *5 large thick slices white crusty bread, about 225 g (8 oz) total weight*
- *butter for greasing*
- *225 g (8 oz) Gruyère cheese, grated*

1 Cook the spinach with just the water clinging to the leaves after washing, for about 4-5 minutes or until wilted. Drain thoroughly, squeezing out as much of the liquid as possible. Chop the spinach.

2 Whisk together the milk, eggs, 45 ml (3 tbsp) Parmesan, the chilli seasoning and nutmeg. Season with salt and pepper. Halve the bread slices if large.

3 Place half the spinach in the base of a well

SWEET POTATO AND LEEK TORTILLA

PREPARATION TIME 10 minutes
COOKING TIME About 20 minutes
FREEZING Not suitable

SERVES 4

- *450 g (1 lb) sweet potato*
- *salt and pepper*
- *60 ml (4 tbsp) olive oil*
- *3 leeks, trimmed, washed and thinly sliced*
- *4 eggs*

525 CALS/SERVING

- *125 ml (4 fl oz) single cream or milk*
- *125 g (4 oz) Gruyère or mature Cheddar cheese, grated*
- *30 ml (2 tbsp) chopped fresh parsley*

1 Peel the sweet potato, and cut into 2.5 cm (1 inch) chunks. Cook in boiling salted water for about 5-8 minutes, until just tender. Drain.
2 Heat the oil in a large frying pan, add the leeks and cook until softened. Add the sweet potato, and cook, stirring occasionally, until the potato is just beginning to colour.
3 Meanwhile, beat the eggs with the cream. Season with salt and pepper, then pour into the frying pan. Add the grated cheese, and stir a little until the cheese is evenly distributed. Cook gently until set on the bottom.
4 Place the omelette under the grill, and cook until puffed up and golden. Serve straight from the pan, sprinkled with the parsley.

VARIATION Use carrots instead of sweet potato.

TIP
This variation of a Spanish tortilla can be served as a tapas-style snack with drinks – allow to cool and cut into neat chunks.

47

PASTA WITH TUNA AND OLIVE SAUCE

PREPARATION TIME 10 minutes, plus soaking
COOKING TIME About 25 minutes
FREEZING Not suitable

SERVES 4

- *50 g (2 oz) can anchovy fillets*
- *milk, for soaking*
- *15 ml (1 tbsp) olive oil*
- *1 onion, peeled and chopped*
- *1 garlic clove, peeled and crushed*
- *5 ml (1 tsp) dried marjoram*
- *400 g (14 oz) can chopped tomatoes*
- *350 g (12 oz) dried pasta shapes*
- *salt and pepper*

490 CALS/SERVING

- *225 g (8 oz) can tuna steaks in brine, well drained and flaked*
- *50 g (2 oz) black or green olives*
- *30 ml (2 tbsp) dry white wine*
- *fresh marjoram, to garnish (optional)*
- *coarsely grated Parmesan cheese, to serve*

1 To remove the salt from the anchovies, drain well and place in a bowl. Cover with milk and soak for 20 minutes. Drain, pat dry and chop.
2 To make the sauce, heat the oil in a saucepan and gently cook the onion for 5 minutes. Add the garlic, marjoram and tomatoes with their juices. Bring to the boil and simmer for 15 minutes, stirring occasionally, until slightly thickened.
3 Meanwhile, cook the pasta in boiling salted water for 10-12 minutes, or until just tender *(al dente)*.
4 Add the tuna fish, anchovies and olives to the sauce. Return to the boil, stirring, then simmer for 2-3 minutes. Stir in the wine and pepper. Drain the pasta and serve hot with the sauce spooned over. Garnish with fresh marjoram, if wished, and top with coarsely grated Parmesan.

SPAGHETTI WITH CLAMS

PREPARATION TIME 15 minutes
COOKING TIME About 8 minutes
FREEZING Not suitable

SERVES 4-6

- *700 g (1½ lb) venus or baby clams in shells*
- *75 ml (5 tbsp) extra-virgin olive oil*
- *3 garlic cloves, peeled and finely chopped*
- *2.5 ml (½ tsp) dried chilli flakes, crushed*
- *350 g (12 oz) tomatoes, skinned, deseeded and chopped*

685-460 CALS/SERVING

- *100 ml (3½ fl oz) dry white wine*
- *salt and pepper*
- *400 g (14 oz) dried spaghetti*
- *30 ml (2 tbsp) chopped fresh parsley*
- *40 g (1½ oz) butter*

1 Wash the clams in plenty of cold water and scrub the shells with a small brush. Leave to soak in a bowl of fresh cold water for 10 minutes, then rinse again and drain well. Discard any clams which do not close if their shells are tapped firmly.
2 Heat the olive oil in a large frying pan (large enough to hold and toss the spaghetti later). Add the garlic and chilli and cook over a medium-high heat for 2 minutes; do not let the garlic brown. Stir in the chopped tomatoes and wine.
3 Add the clams in their shells to the pan. Season with salt and pepper, stir well and bring to the boil. Cover with a tight-fitting lid and cook for 2-3 minutes to steam open the clams. Remove from the heat; discard any clams which have not opened.
4 Meanwhile, cook the spaghetti until just tender *(al dente)*. Drain thoroughly.
5 Return the clam sauce to the heat and stir in the parsley. Add the drained spaghetti and cook for 1 minute. Add the butter, toss lightly and serve.

VARIATIONS When fresh clams are not available, use jars or cans of clams in their shells, available from Italian delicatessens and larger supermarkets. Drain thoroughly before use, and include a few chopped anchovy fillets to taste.
    Alternatively, replace the clams with 1 kg (2 lb) fresh mussels in their shells.

LINGUINE WITH PARMA HAM AND SUN-DRIED TOMATOES

PREPARATION TIME 5 minutes, plus marinating
COOKING TIME 11 minutes
FREEZING Not suitable

SERVES 4
- *400 g (14 oz) dried linguine (or fettucini)*
- *salt and pepper*
- *30 ml (2 tbsp) olive oil*
- *125 g (4 oz) Parma ham (about 6 thin slices), cut into thin strips*
- *65 g (2½ oz) butter*
- *1 large onion, peeled and chopped*
- *2 garlic cloves, peeled and crushed*
- *50 g (2 oz) sun-dried tomatoes, drained and cut into strips*

1020 CALS/SERVING
- *150 ml (5 fl oz) double cream*
- *150 g (5 oz) mascarpone cheese*
- *small bunch of marjoram or oregano sprigs, leaves pulled from stalks*
- *30-45 ml (2-3 tbsp) toasted pine nuts (optional)*

1 Cook the pasta in a large saucepan of boiling, salted water for 10 minutes or until almost tender *(al dente)*.

2 Meanwhile, heat the oil in a frying pan, add the strips of Parma ham and fry quickly for about 1 minute or until frazzled. Using a slotted spoon, remove the ham from the pan and reserve.

3 Add the butter to the frying pan and gently fry the onion, garlic and sun-dried tomatoes for 2 minutes. Drain the pasta, and while still hot, add to the frying pan. With a fork in each hand, lift the pasta strands a few times, so the buttery mixture coats and separates them.

4 In a saucepan, gently heat the cream with the mascarpone, stirring until smooth. Season with salt and pepper, add to the pasta mixture and toss with half the Parma ham and half the marjoram or oregano leaves.

5 Transfer the mixture to a warm serving bowl and scatter with the remaining Parma ham, herbs and toasted pine nuts, if using. Serve at once.

VARIATIONS Use strips of pancetta or smoked streaky bacon instead of Parma ham and cook in the same way. Sautéed sliced mushrooms or asparagus tips also make tasty additions.

CREAMY PASTA BAKE

PREPARATION TIME 15 minutes
COOKING TIME 45 minutes
FREEZING Not suitable

SERVES 4

- *175 g (6 oz) dried pasta shapes, such as penne*
- *salt and pepper*
- *olive oil*
- *125 g (4 oz) onion, peeled and finely chopped*

550 CALS/SERVING

- *1 garlic clove, peeled and crushed*
- *300 ml (10 fl oz) single cream*
- *2 eggs*
- *175 g (6 oz) Gruyère cheese, coarsely grated*

1 Cook the pasta in boiling, salted water until just tender *(al dente)*. Drain well and toss in a little oil.
2 Meanwhile, heat 15 ml (1 tbsp) oil in a small frying pan and add the onion and garlic. Fry for a few minutes until the mixture is beginning to soften.
3 In a large bowl, whisk together the single cream and the eggs; then season generously. Stir in the cheese, the onion mixture and the cooked pasta.
4 Spoon into a 1.1 litre (2 pint) ovenproof dish. Stand the dish on a baking sheet and bake at 190°C (375 °F) mark 5 for 35-40 minutes or until the top is golden brown.

ROASTED VEGETABLE AND PASTA GRATIN

PREPARATION TIME 35 minutes
COOKING TIME 1½ hours
FREEZING Suitable (stage 4)

❋

SERVES 8

- *450 g (1 lb) aubergines, cut into bite-sized pieces*
- *700 g (1½ lb) mixed peppers, deseeded and cut into bite-sized pieces*
- *450 g (1 lb) squash, such as butternut or pumpkin, peeled and cut into bite-sized pieces*
- *90 ml (6 tbsp) olive oil*
- *225 g (8 oz) dried pasta shapes*
- *50 g (2 oz) butter*

585 CALS/SERVING

- *50 g (2 oz) white plain flour*
- *900 ml (1½ pints) milk*
- *30 ml (2 tbsp) wholegrain mustard*
- *150 g (5 oz) soft cheese with garlic and herbs*
- *225 g (8 oz) mature Cheddar cheese, grated*
- *salt and pepper*
- *450 g (1 lb) frozen leaf spinach, thawed and drained*

1 Put the aubergines, mixed peppers and squash into two roasting tins with the oil. Roast at 220°C (425°F) mark 7 for 45 minutes or until tender and charred.

2 Meanwhile, cook the pasta shapes in boiling salted water until just tender *(al dente)*. Drain them thoroughly.

3 Melt the butter in a pan and then stir in the flour. Cook, stirring, for 1 minute before adding the milk. Bring to the boil, stirring all the time. Simmer for 2-3 minutes or until the sauce thickens. Off the heat, add the mustard, soft cheese and all but 50 g (2 oz) of the Cheddar. Stir thoroughly until smooth. Season well.

4 Mix the pasta, spinach and roasted vegetables with the sauce. Spoon the vegetable and pasta gratin into a large, shallow ovenproof dish and sprinkle over the remaining Cheddar cheese.

5 Stand the dish on a baking sheet and cook at 200°C (400°F) mark 6 for about 40 minutes or until hot and golden brown, covering with foil, if necessary, to prevent over browning.

VARIATIONS This dish is a great way of using up leftovers. You can add cooked ham, chicken or spicy sausage. Any variety of cheese can be used; for a special vegetarian meal, add goats' cheese or Stilton.

PAD THAI NOODLES

PREPARATION TIME 15 minutes
COOKING TIME 5 minutes
FREEZING Not suitable

🕐

SERVES 4   615 CALS/SERVING

- *250 g (9 oz) flat, thin rice or egg noodles*
- *30 ml (2 tbsp) sesame oil*
- *125 g (4 oz) turnip, diced*
- *2 garlic cloves, peeled and crushed*
- *2.5 ml (½ tsp) hot paprika*
- *60-75 ml (4-5 tbsp) fish sauce*
- *juice of 1 lime*
- *15 ml (1 tbsp) tomato purée*

- *125 g (4 oz) tofu, diced*
- *50 g (2 oz) roasted peanuts, finely chopped*
- *125 g (4 oz) cooked, peeled prawns*
- *175 g (6 oz) beansprouts*
- *2 eggs, beaten*
- *chopped peanuts, to serve*
- *whole cooked prawns and basil, to garnish*

1 Cook the noodles according to the packet instructions. Heat the oil in a wok or large non-stick sauté pan. Add the noodles, turnip, garlic and paprika and sauté for 1-2 minutes, stirring to prevent the noodles from sticking. Add the fish sauce, lime juice and tomato purée and cook for a further 1 minute, stirring continuously.

2 Stir in the tofu, peanuts, prawns and beansprouts. Lower the heat, add the eggs and stir for about 1 minute or until the noodles are coated in lightly cooked egg. Serve sprinkled with chopped peanuts and garnished with prawns and basil.

> *TIP*
> Work quickly and merely toss the ingredients in the pan to heat them through and lightly cook the egg.

1 To make the rouille, place the pepper, garlic and chilli in a food processor or blender with the oil and breadcrumbs and blend to a smooth paste. Transfer to a small serving dish.

2 To make the stew, heat the oil in a large saucepan. Add the leeks, ginger, orange rind and bay leaves and fry for 3 minutes. Add the stock and potatoes and bring to the boil. Reduce the heat and simmer gently for 10 minutes or until the potatoes are almost tender.

3 Add the red pepper, courgettes, mushrooms, kidney beans and saffron. Cover and simmer gently for 10-15 minutes until all the vegetables are tender but not pulpy. Add the cream and season to taste.

4 Spoon into large bowls or onto plates and serve with the rouille handed separately.

VEGETABLE STEW WITH ROUILLE

PREPARATION TIME 30 minutes
COOKING TIME 28 minutes
FREEZING Not suitable

SERVES 4   600 CALS/SERVING

- 45 ml (3 tbsp) olive oil
- 2 large leeks, trimmed and sliced
- 2.5 cm (1 inch) piece fresh root ginger, peeled and grated
- piece of pared orange rind
- 2 bay leaves
- 900 ml (1½ pints) vegetable stock
- 450 g (1 lb) small whole potatoes, scrubbed and halved, if necessary
- 1 red pepper, deseeded and chopped
- 225 g (8 oz) courgettes or green beans, sliced
- 225 g (8 oz) brown mushrooms, halved
- 400 g (14 oz) can red kidney beans, drained and rinsed
- generous pinch (½ sachet) saffron strands (optional)
- 60 ml (4 tbsp) double cream
- salt and pepper
ROUILLE
- 1 red pepper, deseeded and roughly chopped
- 4 garlic cloves, peeled and chopped
- 1 fresh chilli, deseeded and chopped, or 2.5 ml (½ tsp) crushed dried chillies
- 75 ml (5 tbsp) olive oil
- 25 g (1 oz) fresh breadcrumbs

MIXED VEGETABLES AND TOFU IN COCONUT SAUCE

PREPARATION TIME 20 minutes
COOKING TIME About 30 minutes
FREEZING Not suitable

SERVES 4   365 CALS/SERVING

- 75 g (3 oz) creamed coconut, cut into small pieces
- 225 g (8 oz) tofu, cut into cubes
- sunflower oil, for deep-frying, plus 15 ml (1 tbsp)
- 6 spring onions, finely chopped
- 2.5 cm (1 inch) piece fresh root ginger, peeled and finely chopped
- 1 garlic clove, peeled and crushed
- 2.5 ml (½ tsp) ground turmeric
- 2.5 ml (½ tsp) chilli powder
- 30 ml (2 tbsp) soy sauce
- 4 carrots, cut into matchstick strips
- 225 g (8 oz) cauliflower florets, separated into small sprigs
- 175 g (6 oz) French beans
- 175 g (6 oz) beansprouts
- salt and pepper

1 Place the coconut in a measuring jug. Pour in boiling water to the 900 ml (1½ pint) mark. Stir until dissolved, then strain through a muslin-lined sieve. Set the milk aside.

2 Pat the tofu dry with absorbent kitchen paper. Heat the oil to 190°C (375°F) in a wok or deep-

fat fryer, and deep-fry the tofu until golden, turning frequently. Remove and drain on absorbent kitchen paper.

3 Heat the 15 ml (1 tbsp) oil in a saucepan or flameproof casserole and gently fry the spring onions, ginger and garlic for about 5 minutes until soft.

4 Add the turmeric and chilli powder. Stir-fry for 1-2 minutes. Pour in the coconut milk and soy sauce and bring to the boil, stirring. Add the carrots and cauliflower and simmer, uncovered, for 10 minutes.

5 Add the French beans and simmer for a further 5 minutes before adding the tofu and beansprouts. Heat through and adjust the seasoning, then turn into a warmed serving dish. Serve immediately.

CRUSTY MEDITERRANEAN PARCELS

PREPARATION TIME 30 minutes, plus pastry
COOKING TIME 1 hour 10 minutes
FREEZING Suitable (stage 5)

SERVES 8

- *700 g (1½ lb) mixed vegetables, such as carrots, leeks, courgettes, red peppers, aubergines, sweet potatoes, cut into 2.5 cm (1 inch) chunks*
- *30 ml (2 tbsp) olive oil*
- *salt and pepper*
- *225 g (8 oz) onions, peeled and roughly chopped*
- *2 garlic cloves, peeled and crushed*
- *400 g (14 oz) can chopped tomatoes*

480 CALS/SERVING

- *15 ml (1 tbsp) sun-dried tomato paste*
- *125 g (4 oz) Gruyère cheese, grated*
- *200 g (7 oz) mascarpone cheese*
- *50 ml (2 fl oz) single cream*
- *30 ml (2 tbsp) finely chopped fresh chives*
- *50 g (2 oz) pine nuts, toasted*
- *450 g (1 lb) Puff Pastry (see page 75)*
- *1 egg*
- *chopped fresh chives, to garnish*

1 Place the vegetables in a small roasting tin with 15 ml (1 tbsp) olive oil and seasoning. Cook at 200°C (400°F) mark 6 for 40-45 minutes or until just tender, stirring occasionally. Remove from the oven and leave to cool.

2 Heat the remaining olive oil in a frying pan. Add the onions and garlic and fry for 5 minutes

or until lightly coloured. Add the tomatoes and tomato paste and simmer, uncovered, for 15-20 minutes or until thick and pulpy. Set aside.

3 Mix 75 g (3 oz) Gruyère cheese with the mascarpone cheese, single cream and chives. Mix the vegetables with the tomato sauce, 25 g (1 oz) pine nuts and seasoning. Roll out the pastry quite thinly to 2 rectangles measuring about 35 x 30 cm (14 x 12 inches).

4 Beat the egg with a pinch of salt. Place half the vegetables down the centre of each oblong, about 10 cm (4 inches) wide. Top the vegetables with the cheese mixture. Brush the pastry with the egg glaze.

5 With a sharp knife, make diagonal incisions about 2.5 cm (1 inch) apart, down each side of the filling to within 2.5 cm (1 inch) of the filling. Plait from the top by overlapping alternate strips from either side across the filling. Make sure that the strips cross over or the pastry might burst in cooking. Tuck any loose pastry under the base. Brush liberally with the egg glaze and sprinkle with pepper, salt, the remaining grated cheese and pine nuts.

6 Place the plaits on a baking sheet. Cook at 220°C (425°F) mark 7 for 25 minutes or until golden brown. Cover loosely with foil if they begin to brown too quickly.

7 Serve cut into slices and sprinkled with chopped chives.

BAKED CABBAGE WITH FRUITED BULGHUR WHEAT STUFFING

PREPARATION TIME 30 minutes
COOKING TIME 40-45 minutes
FREEZING Not suitable

SERVES 4

- *8 large green cabbage leaves*
- *125 g (4 oz) bulghur wheat*
- *30 ml (2 tbsp) olive oil*
- *2 large onions, peeled and sliced*
- *50 g (2 oz) hazelnuts, roughly chopped*
- *1 garlic clove, peeled and crushed*
- *175 g (6 oz) carrots, peeled and diced*
- *50 g (2 oz) no-soak dried apricots, roughly chopped*

355 CALS/SERVING

- *10 ml (2 tsp) coriander seeds, lightly crushed*
- *45 ml (3 tbsp) chopped fresh parsley*
- *25 g (1 oz) raisins*
- *salt and pepper*
- *10 ml (2 tsp) white plain flour*
- *450 ml (15 fl oz) vegetable stock*
- *coriander or parsley, to garnish*

1 Cut the stalks away from the cabbage leaves. Bring a large pan of water to the boil and cook the leaves for 1-2 minutes until softened. Drain.
2 Put the bulghur wheat in a bowl and cover with boiling water. Leave for 10 minutes until softened, then drain.

3 Heat the oil in a large frying pan. Add the onions and fry for about 8-10 minutes until turning golden brown, adding the hazelnuts after 5 minutes of cooking. Drain and reserve three-quarters of the mixture.
4 Add the garlic, carrots, apricots, bulghur wheat, coriander, parsley and raisins to the pan. Stir well and season to taste.
5 Spoon the stuffing onto the cabbage leaves. Fold two sides of the leaves over the filling and then roll up to enclose completely. (If they start to unroll, secure with cocktail sticks.)
6 Place the reserved onion mixture in a flame-proof casserole over moderate heat. Blend in the flour, then the stock. Bring to the boil and season lightly. Place the cabbage parcels in the casserole in a single layer.
7 Cover with a lid and bake at 200°C (400°F) mark 6 for 30 minutes. Carefully remove the parcels. Using a slotted spoon, transfer the onions and nuts to warmed serving plates. Top with the parcels and pour over the pan juices. Serve scattered with coriander or parsley.

VARIATIONS Use prunes in place of the apricots. Any other nuts, such as brazil nuts, almonds or walnuts can be used instead of hazelnuts.

VEGETABLE BIRYANI

PREPARATION TIME 20 minutes
COOKING TIME 45 minutes
FREEZING Not suitable

SERVES 4

- *350 g (12 oz) basmati rice*
- *salt and pepper*
- *50 g (2 oz) ghee or clarified butter*
- *1 large onion, peeled and chopped*
- *2.5 cm (1 inch) piece fresh root ginger, peeled and grated*
- *1-2 garlic cloves, peeled and crushed*
- *5 ml (1 tsp) ground coriander*
- *10 ml (2 tsp) ground cumin*

485 CALS/SERVING

- *5 ml (1 tsp) ground turmeric*
- *2.5 ml (½ tsp) chilli powder*
- *3 carrots, peeled and thinly sliced*
- *225 g (8 oz) French beans, halved*
- *225 g (8 oz) small cauliflower florets*
- *5 ml (1 tsp) garam masala*
- *juice of 1 lemon*
- *hard-boiled egg slices and coriander sprigs, to garnish*

1 Put the rice in a sieve and rinse under cold running water until the water runs clear.

2 Put the rice in a saucepan with 600 ml (1 pint) water and 5 ml (1 tsp) salt. Bring to the boil, then reduce the heat and simmer for 10 minutes or until only just tender.

3 Meanwhile, melt the ghee or butter in a large heavy-based saucepan, add the onion, ginger and garlic and fry gently for 5 minutes or until soft but not coloured. Add the coriander, cumin, turmeric and chilli powder and fry for 2 minutes more, stirring constantly to prevent the spices burning.

4 Remove the rice from the heat and drain. Add 900 ml (1½ pints) water to the onion and spice mixture and season with salt and pepper. Stir well and bring to the boil. Add the carrots and beans and simmer for 15 minutes, then add the cauliflower and simmer for a further 10 minutes. Lastly, add the rice. Mix gently and heat through.

5 Stir the garam masala and lemon juice into the biryani and simmer for a few minutes. Taste and adjust the seasoning, then turn into a warmed dish. Garnish with egg and coriander and serve.

SPICED VEGETABLE TAGINE

PREPARATION TIME 15 minutes
COOKING TIME 40 minutes
FREEZING Suitable (stage 4) without couscous

SERVES 4

- *225 g (8 oz) couscous*
- *60 ml (4 tbsp) olive oil*
- *2 garlic cloves, peeled and crushed*
- *2.5 ml (½ tsp) chilli flakes*
- *1 onion, peeled and chopped*
- *10 ml (2 tsp) ground coriander*
- *10 ml (2 tsp) paprika*
- *5 ml (1 tsp) each ground cumin, turmeric and cinnamon*
- *2 medium potatoes, peeled and cubed*

560 CALS/SERVING

- *2 large carrots, peeled and sliced*
- *225 g (8 oz) celeriac, peeled and cubed*
- *400 g (14 oz) can chick-peas*
- *300 ml (10 fl oz) tomato juice*
- *30 ml (2 tbsp) tomato purée*
- *15 ml (1 tbsp) chilli sauce*
- *125 g (4 oz) sultanas*
- *salt and pepper*
- *45 ml (3 tbsp) chopped fresh coriander*

1 Place the couscous in a sieve and wash under cold running water to moisten all the grains, turn out onto a baking sheet and spread out to the sides. Leave until required.

2 Heat the oil in a saucepan and fry the garlic, chilli flakes, onion and spices for 10 minutes. Add the potatoes, carrots and celeriac and continue to fry gently for a further 5 minutes.

3 Stir in the chick-peas with their liquid, together with the tomato juice, tomato purée and chilli sauce. Bring to the boil. Cover, reduce the heat slightly and simmer for 20 minutes.

4 Stir in the sultanas and cook, covered, for a further 10 minutes.

5 Meanwhile, cook the couscous according to the packet instructions. Season the stew to taste, stir in the chopped coriander and serve with the couscous and extra chilli sauce, if wished.

VARIATION For meat eaters, lamb makes a delicious addition to this stew. Cube 450 g (1 lb) lean lamb, seal the meat in hot fat until well browned, then add the garlic, onions and spices and continue as above.

TIP
If you possess a double boiler, steam the couscous over the stew which will impart a lovely flavour to the couscous as it cooks.

RED CABBAGE WITH PINE NUTS

PREPARATION TIME 10 minutes
COOKING TIME About 25 minutes
FREEZING Not suitable
♡

SERVES 8

- *25 ml (1 fl oz) olive oil*
- *900 g (2 lb) red cabbage, finely shredded*
- *2.5 cm (1 inch) piece fresh root ginger, peeled and grated (optional)*
- *150 ml (5 fl oz) light stock*

135 CALS/SERVING

- *salt and pepper*
- *40 g (1½ oz) butter*
- *30 ml (2 tbsp) balsamic vinegar or red wine vinegar plus 10 ml (2 tsp) muscovado sugar*
- *50 g (2 oz) toasted pine nuts*

1 Heat the oil in a large saucepan and sauté the cabbage with the ginger, if using, over a high heat for 3-4 minutes or until reduced in bulk, stirring occasionally.

2 Add the stock and seasoning, bring to the boil, then cover and cook over a low heat for about 20 minutes. Stir occasionally.

3 When the cabbage is just tender, uncover and bubble down any excess liquid. Off the heat, stir in the butter, balsamic vinegar and pine nuts. Adjust the seasoning and serve.

CITRUS LEEKS WITH SUGAR SNAP PEAS

PREPARATION TIME 15 minutes
COOKING TIME 10-15 minutes
FREEZING Not suitable
♡ ⏱

SERVES 6

- 20-30 ml (1½-2 tbsp) olive oil
- 700 g (1½ lb) trimmed leeks, cut into 1 cm (½ inch) slices
- 450 g (1 lb) sugar snap peas or mangetouts, topped and tailed
- salt and pepper
DRESSING
- 45 ml (3 tbsp) olive oil

150 CALS/SERVING

- 15 ml (1 tbsp) balsamic vinegar
- 2.5 ml (½ tsp) soft light brown sugar
- 10-15 ml (2-3 tsp) lemon juice
- 2.5 ml (½ tsp) Dijon mustard
- grated rind and juice of ½ orange

1 Heat the oil in a large sauté pan. Add the leeks and sauté gently for 5-6 minutes or until just tender. Cook the sugar snap peas in boiling salted water for 5 minutes. Drain, then mix with the leeks.
2 Mix together all the dressing ingredients and season with salt and pepper to taste. Stir into the hot vegetables and serve at once.

> *TIP*
> This dish can also be served cold as a tangy salad accompaniment to cold turkey.

CHESTNUT AND SPROUT SAUTE

PREPARATION TIME 15-25 minutes
COOKING TIME 15-45 minutes
FREEZING Not suitable

SERVES 8

- 900 g (2 lb) fresh chestnuts or 875 g (1 lb 15 oz) can whole chestnuts
- 600 ml (1 pint) chicken stock
- 900 g (2 lb) Brussels sprouts, trimmed
- salt and pepper

350 CALS/SERVING

- 450 g (1 lb) onions
- 125 g (4 oz) butter
- 225 g (8 oz) celery, cut into 2.5 cm (1 inch) pieces
- grated rind of 1 lemon
- chopped fresh parsley, to garnish

1 If using fresh chestnuts, nick the brown outer skins with a sharp knife. Cook in boiling water for 10 minutes. Drain, cool and peel off the shells and inner skins. Cover with the stock and simmer for 20 minutes or until tender. Drain the chestnuts well.
2 Cook the sprouts in boiling, salted water for 3-4 minutes only, then drain well. Peel the onions, then quarter them and separate the layers.
3 Melt the butter in a large sauté or frying pan. Sauté the celery and onions with the lemon rind until beginning to soften.
4 Add the cooked chestnuts, Brussels sprouts and seasoning. Sauté over a high heat for a further 2-3 minutes or until piping hot, stirring frequently. Cover and keep warm until ready to serve, then sprinkle with chopped parsley to garnish.

PARSNIPS IN A LIME GLAZE

PREPARATION TIME 5 minutes
COOKING TIME 17 minutes
FREEZING Not suitable

⏱

SERVES 4
- *700 g (1½ lb) parsnips, peeled*
- *salt and pepper*
- *1 lime*
- *50 g (2 oz) butter*

225 CALS/SERVING
- *25 g (1 oz) light muscovado sugar*
- *thyme sprigs, to garnish*

1 Cut the parsnips in half lengthways. (If using older, tougher parsnips, cut into quarters and remove the woody cores.) Add to a pan of boiling salted water and cook for 5 minutes.
2 Meanwhile, using a vegetable peeler, pare thin slivers of rind from the lime, then set aside for the garnish. Halve the lime and squeeze out the juice.
3 Melt the butter in a large saucepan together with the sugar. Add the lime juice and heat gently,

stirring, to dissolve the sugar.
4 Drain the parsnips, then add to the lime mixture in the pan. Toss in the buttery lime mixture and cook over a moderate heat, shaking the pan frequently, for about 10 minutes until golden brown.
5 Transfer to a warmed serving dish and garnish with the slivers of lime rind and thyme sprigs.

VARIATIONS The sharp glaze can be used with any sweet root vegetable to excellent effect – try it with sweet potatoes or carrots. A handful of walnuts tossed in towards the end of the cooking time adds a delicious crunch.

AROMATIC SWEDE AND CARROTS

PREPARATION TIME 20 minutes
COOKING TIME 15 minutes
FREEZING Not suitable
♡

SERVES 4

- *450 g (1 lb) swede, peeled and diced*
- *450 g (1 lb) carrots, peeled and thinly sliced*
- *salt and pepper*
- *25 g (1 oz) butter*

105 CALS/SERVING

- *5 ml (1 tsp) black mustard seeds*
- *2 pieces preserved stem ginger in syrup, drained*
- *parsley or chervil sprigs, to garnish*

1 Cook the vegetables separately in boiling salted water until tender.
2 Meanwhile, melt the butter in a small heavy-based saucepan. Add the mustard seeds and heat gently until the seeds begin to pop. Add the chopped ginger and cook for 1 minute over a low heat.
3 Drain the cooked swede and carrots thoroughly, then mash together using a potato masher or vegetable mill. Season generously with pepper and stir in half of the mustard and ginger mixture.
4 Transfer the mashed swede and carrots to a warmed serving dish and drizzle the remaining mustard and ginger mixture over the top. Garnish with parsley or chervil and serve at once.

POTATO AND CELERIAC GALETTE

PREPARATION TIME 25 minutes
COOKING TIME 1¼ hours
FREEZING Not suitable
♡

SERVES 4

- *450 g (1 lb) old potatoes, peeled*
- *450 g (1 lb) celeriac, peeled*
- *1 garlic clove, peeled and crushed*
- *freshly grated nutmeg*

150 CALS/SERVING

- *salt and pepper*
- *25 g (1 oz) butter, melted*
- *chopped fresh parsley, to garnish*

1 Grease and base-line a 20 cm (8 inch) sandwich tin with non-stick baking parchment.
2 Very thinly slice the potatoes and celeriac, preferably in a food processor.
3 Layer up the vegetables with the garlic, nutmeg and seasoning, pressing down firmly as you go. Pour the melted butter over the vegetables.
4 Cover with foil and bake at 230°C (450°F) mark 8 for 1¼ hours or until the vegetables are quite tender. Test with a skewer.
5 Turn the galette out onto a serving plate and garnish with parsley.

GOLDEN POTATOES

PREPARATION TIME 5 minutes
COOKING TIME 1½ hours
FREEZING Not suitable

SERVES 6

- *1.1 kg (2½ lb) old potatoes*
- *salt and pepper*
- *2 sprigs rosemary*

230 CALS/SERVING

- *6 garlic cloves (optional)*
- *45 ml (3 tbsp) olive oil*

1 Wash the potatoes and cut into large chunks, but do not peel. Place in cold, salted water, bring to the boil and simmer for 3 minutes. Drain the potatoes well. Strip the spiky rosemary leaves off the sprigs.
2 Place the potatoes in a roasting tin with the unpeeled garlic cloves, if using, rosemary and olive oil.
3 Roast at 200°C (400°F) mark 6 for 1½ hours, basting and turning a few times.

SWEET AND HOT GREEN BEANS WITH PEANUTS

PREPARATION TIME 15 minutes
COOKING TIME About 10 minutes
FREEZING Not suitable
♡ ⏱

SERVES 4-6   200-135 CALS/SERVING
- *450 g (1 lb) French beans, topped*
- *30 ml (2 tbsp) vegetable oil*
- *1 onion, peeled, halved and cut into thin slivers*
- *6 dried red chillies, finely chopped*
- *2 garlic cloves, peeled and crushed*
- *15 ml (1 tbsp) dark soy sauce*
- *30 ml (2 tbsp) clear honey*
- *50 g (2 oz) unsalted roasted peanuts*

1 Blanch the beans in a pan of boiling water for 2 minutes. Drain and refresh the beans under cold water, then drain well again.
2 Heat the oil in a wok or large frying pan, add the beans, onion, chillies and garlic and stir-fry for 2 minutes. Add the soy sauce and the honey, reduce the heat, cover and cook for 3 minutes.
3 Uncover and cook until the liquid thickens, turning the beans to coat them in the honey and soy mixture. Sprinkle with the nuts and serve.

SPICY MUSHROOMS

PREPARATION TIME 10 minutes
COOKING TIME 45 minutes
FREEZING Not suitable
♡

SERVES 6   180 CALS/SERVING
- *oil for frying*
- *1 large aubergine, about 350 g (12 oz), cut into chunks*
- *3 garlic cloves, peeled and crushed*
- *2 large onions, about 450 g (1 lb), peeled and finely sliced*
- *5 cm (2 inch) piece fresh root ginger, peeled and coarsely grated*
- *10 ml (2 tsp) hot chilli powder*
- *5 ml (1 tsp) turmeric*
- *5 ml (1 tsp) garam masala*
- *5 ml (1 tsp) cumin*
- *two 400 g (14 oz) cans chopped tomatoes*
- *salt and pepper*
- *350 g (12 oz) button mushrooms, halved*
- *225 g (8 oz) frozen peas*

1 Heat about 60 ml (4 tbsp) oil in a large, non-stick frying pan. Fry the aubergine pieces until golden brown, adding more oil if necessary. Remove the aubergine from the pan and drain on absorbent kitchen paper. Add a little more oil to the pan if necessary then add the garlic, onions and ginger. Cook until golden, stirring occasionally. Mix in the spices and cook for 1 minute, stirring all the time.
2 Return the aubergine to the pan with the tomatoes. Adjust the seasoning then bring to the boil, cover and simmer for about 20 minutes or until the aubergines are tender.
3 Stir in the mushrooms and frozen peas and cook for about a further 10 minutes, adding a little water if necessary to thin down slightly. Transfer to a heated serving dish.

TIP
Hot chilli powder is a blend of chilli, cumin, salt, garlic and oregano. It can be found on the spice racks in supermarkets. Don't be tempted to use pure ground chillies as they are too hot for this recipe.

BUCKWHEAT AND LENTIL PILAFF

PREPARATION TIME 10 minutes, plus soaking
COOKING TIME 30 minutes
FREEZING Not suitable

SERVES 8

- *250 g (9 oz) green lentils*
- *250 g (9 oz) buckwheat*
- *10 ml (2 tsp) ground cinnamon*
- *10 ml (2 tsp) ground coriander*
- *5 ml (1 tsp) salt*
- *12 rashers streaky bacon, cut into 2.5 cm (1 inch) strips*
- *450 g (1 lb) onions, peeled and finely sliced*

335 CALS/SERVING

- *3 garlic cloves, peeled and crushed*
- *olive oil*
- *60 ml (4 tbsp) chopped fresh parsley*
- *60 ml (4 tbsp) chopped fresh coriander*
- *black pepper*
- *150 ml (5 fl oz) soured cream and ground cinnamon, to serve*

1 Soak the lentils and the buckwheat separately in bowls of cold water for 1 hour.
2 Drain the lentils and the buckwheat and place the lentils in a saucepan with 900 ml (1½ pints) water, the spices and salt and bring to the boil. Cook, uncovered, for about 20 minutes or until all the liquid has been absorbed and the lentils are tender. Boil the buckwheat for about 15 minutes, then drain. Mix the lentils and buckwheat together.
3 In a non-stick frying pan, fry the bacon until crispy and drain on absorbent kitchen paper. Add the onion and garlic to the pan and fry until golden brown, adding a little oil if necessary.
4 Add the bacon and the onion mixture to the lentils and buckwheat. Stir in the parsley and coriander, then mix in 30 ml (2 tbsp) oil. Season to taste. Serve warm or cold, topped with soured cream and sprinkled with cinnamon.

WINTER SALAD

PREPARATION TIME 20 minutes
FREEZING Not suitable

SERVES 4

- *1 lemon*
- *30 ml (2 tbsp) olive oil*
- *150 ml (5 fl oz) natural yogurt*
- *salt and pepper*
- *2 eating apples*
- *225 g (8 oz) red cabbage, thinly sliced*
- *1 small onion, peeled and thinly sliced*

340 CALS/SERVING

- *4 celery sticks, trimmed and thinly sliced*
- *125 g (4 oz) Cheddar cheese, cut into cubes*
- *50 g (2 oz) unsalted peanuts in skins*
- *celery leaves, to garnish (optional)*

1 In a large bowl whisk together the grated rind of half the lemon, 45 ml (3 tbsp) lemon juice, the olive oil and yogurt. Season well.
2 Core and roughly chop the apples, then toss in the dressing.
3 Toss all the ingredients, except the peanuts and celery leaves, with the apples, mixing well. Sprinkle with peanuts and garnish with celery leaves, if liked.

of muslin and tie with string, allowing room for expansion.

4 Tie the puddings onto skewers and hang them over a large pan of boiling water. Tightly cover the pan with foil and steam for about 1½ hours, topping the pan up with more boiling water, if necessary.

5 While the puddings are warm, mould into neat rounds. Hang in a cool place until quite dry. Overwrap in foil and refrigerate for up to a week.

6 To serve, remove the foil and steam, as above, for about 1 hour. Decorate with frosted holly leaves and serve with brandy sauce.

LIGHT CHRISTMAS PUDDINGS

PREPARATION TIME 40 minutes, plus steeping and drying
COOKING TIME 2½ hours
FREEZING Suitable (stage 5)

❄

SERVES 8

- 225 g (8 oz) sultanas, roughly chopped
- 150 g (5 oz) raisins, roughly chopped
- 50 g (2 oz) stoned dates, chopped
- 50 g (2 oz) currants, roughly chopped
- 25 g (1 oz) no-soak dried apricots, roughly chopped
- 1 small eating apple (preferably Granny Smith), peeled and coarsely grated
- grated rind of 1 lemon
- 50 ml (2 fl oz) brandy

445 CALS/PUDDING

- 125 g (4 oz) butter, softened
- 125 g (4 oz) soft dark brown sugar
- 2 small eggs, beaten
- 125 g (4 oz) fresh white breadcrumbs
- 40 g (1½ oz) white plain flour
- 1.25 ml (¼ tsp) each of ground nutmeg and ground cinnamon
- 2.5 ml (½ tsp) bicarbonate of soda
- frosted holly leaves, to decorate
- brandy sauce, to serve

1 Mix the dried fruit with the apple, lemon rind and brandy. Cover and leave in a cool place for two days.

2 Beat the butter and sugar until light and fluffy, then gradually beat in the eggs. Add the fruit mixture with the remaining ingredients and mix.

3 Divide the mixture among eight 25 cm (10 inch) squares of well-floured muslin. Draw up the edges

BREAD AND BUTTER PUDDING WITH PRUNES

PREPARATION TIME 10 minutes, plus soaking
COOKING TIME 1-1¼ hours
FREEZING Not suitable

SERVES 6

- 25 g (1 oz) butter
- 4 slices brown bread, about 150 g (5 oz)
- 3 eggs
- 25 g (1 oz) caster sugar
- 150 ml (5 fl oz) single cream
- 450 ml (15 fl oz) skimmed milk

285 CALS/SERVING

- 15 ml (1 tbsp) brandy
- 125 g (4 oz) pitted no-soak prunes, finely chopped
- 1.25 ml (¼ tsp) ground cinnamon
- 25 g (1 oz) demerara sugar

1 Lightly butter a 7.5 cm (3 inches) deep 1.1 litre (2 pint) ovenproof dish. Spread one side of the bread with the remaining butter. Cut into 2.5 cm (1 inch) squares. Whisk together the eggs, sugar, cream, milk and brandy.

2 Scatter the bread and prunes into the prepared dish. Pour the egg mixture over. Leave to soak for about 20 minutes, lightly pressing the bread into the egg mixture. Sprinkle with the cinnamon and demerara sugar.

3 Place the dish in a roasting tin with enough warm water to come about 2.5 cm (1 inch) up the side of the dish. Cook at 170°C (325°F) mark 3 for about 1 hour-1¼ hours or until the pudding is lightly set. Serve immediately.

STICKY FUDGE AND WALNUT PUDDING

PREPARATION TIME 15 minutes
COOKING TIME 50 minutes
FREEZING Not suitable

SERVES 6

- *150 g (5 oz) butter, plus extra for greasing*
- *175 g (6 oz) soft light brown sugar*
- *300 ml (10 fl oz) double cream*
- *125 g (4 oz) chopped dates*

660 CALS/SERVING

- *2.5 ml (½ tsp) bicarbonate of soda*
- *1 egg, beaten*
- *125 g (4 oz) white self-raising flour*
- *50 g (2 oz) chopped walnuts*

1 Butter a 1.1 litre (2 pint) deep, ovenproof dish. In a saucepan gently warm 75 g (3 oz) butter, 125 g (4 oz) soft light brown sugar and the double cream. Bring the mixture up to a vigorous boil and bubble for about 3 minutes. Pour a little of the fudge sauce into the prepared dish just to cover the base.

2 Put the dates in a small bowl and pour over 125 ml (4 fl oz) boiling water, add the bicarbonate of soda and leave to stand for 10 minutes.

3 In a bowl, beat the remaining sugar with 50 g (2 oz) butter until light and fluffy. Beat in the egg with the date mixture – it will look slightly curdled. Stir in the flour and nuts. Pour into the dish.

4 Bake at 180°C (350°F) mark 4 for about 50 minutes or until firm to the touch. Cool for 5 minutes, run a palette knife around the edge of the dish, then turn out. Warm the remaining fudge sauce and pour over the pudding.

4 Pour into a deep 1.1 litre (2 pint) ovenproof dish. Place in a roasting tin filled with hot water and bake at 180°C (350°F) mark 4 for about 1 hour or until the pudding is very firm to the touch, but still slightly runny underneath. Cover loosely with foil after about 40 minutes to prevent overbrowning, if necessary. Dust with cocoa powder to decorate and serve with ice cream.

APPLE AND WALNUT FILO PIE

PREPARATION TIME 25 minutes
COOKING TIME 50 minutes
FREEZING Not suitable

SERVES 6   425 CALS/SERVING

- *50 g (2 oz) walnut pieces*
- *125 g (4 oz) butter, softened*
- *50 g (2 oz) caster sugar, plus 30 ml (2 tbsp)*
- *finely grated rind and juice of 1 lemon*
- *1 egg*
- *25 g (1 oz) white self-raising flour*
- *2.5 ml (½ tsp) ground cinnamon*
- *700 g (1½ lb) crisp eating apples, peeled and sliced*
- *300 g (10 oz) packet filo pastry*
- *icing sugar, to dust*

1 Toast the walnuts. Allow to cool, then finely chop in a food processor.
2 Beat half the butter with 50 g (2 oz) caster sugar, the lemon rind, egg, flour, half the cinnamon and the chopped walnuts.
3 Mix the apples together with 30 ml (2 tbsp) caster sugar, 15 ml (1 tbsp) lemon juice and the remaining cinnamon.
4 Melt the remaining butter and grease a 25 cm (10 inch) loose-based, fluted flan tin. Use about three-quarters of the pastry to line the tin, buttering well after each piece of pastry and allowing about 7.5 cm (3 inches) of pastry to hang over the sides of the tin.
5 Spread the nut mixture over the pastry base and top with the apples. Fold the pastry edges over the filling and top with a little more pastry to cover the filling completely. Butter between the pastry layers as before. Crumple up any remaining pastry and scatter over the pie. Drizzle with butter.
6 Stand the tin on a baking sheet and bake at 190°C (375°F) mark 5 for about 50 minutes, covering loosely with foil when well browned.
7 Serve warm, dusted with icing sugar.

GOOEY CHOCOLATE PUDDING

PREPARATION TIME 15 minutes
COOKING TIME 1 hour 10 minutes
FREEZING Not suitable

SERVES 4   570 CALS/SERVING

- *200 g (7 oz) milk chocolate*
- *200 ml (7 fl oz) milk*
- *50 g (2 oz) butter, softened*
- *75 g (3 oz) caster sugar*
- *2 eggs, separated*
- *50 g (2 oz) white self-raising flour*
- *25 g (1 oz) cocoa powder*
- *extra cocoa powder, to decorate*
- *vanilla ice cream, to serve*

1 Break the chocolate into small pieces, place in a saucepan with the milk and heat very slowly until all the chocolate has melted. Stir until smooth.
2 Cream together the butter and sugar until light and fluffy. Keep beating and gradually add the egg yolks, chocolate mixture, flour and cocoa powder.
3 In a separate bowl, whisk the egg whites until they hold their shape. Gently fold into the chocolate with a metal spoon.

TIP
The egg whites should stand in soft peaks so that the tips of the peaks flop over gently when held up by the whisk. Overbeaten egg whites will be difficult to fold in evenly.

RAISIN AND ORANGE
CUSTARD TART

PREPARATION TIME 25 minutes, plus chilling
COOKING TIME 1 hour
FREEZING Not suitable

SERVES 8
- *finely grated rind and juice of 1 orange*
- *about 250 ml (8 fl oz) fresh orange juice*
- *325 g (11 oz) raisins, preferably the large Lexia variety*
- *225 g (8 oz) white plain flour*

450 CALS/SERVING
- *150 g (5 oz) butter*
- *75 g (3 oz) icing sugar*
- *2 egg yolks plus 3 whole eggs*
- *450 ml (15 fl oz) milk or double cream, or milk and cream mixed*

1 Strain the juice from the orange and make up to 300 ml (10 fl oz) with the fresh orange juice. Place in a saucepan with the raisins and simmer until all the liquid has evaporated.
2 Meanwhile, place the flour, butter, icing sugar, egg yolks and 15 ml (1 tbsp) water in a food processor and blend until the mixture resembles a crumble topping. Press into the base and up the sides of a 23 cm (9 inch) round 4 cm (1½ inch) deep, loose-based, fluted flan tin. Chill for 45 minutes.

3 Bake blind (see page 383) at 200°C (400°F) mark 6 for 15 minutes or until the edges have turned golden brown. Remove the beans and paper. Reduce the oven temperature to 180°C (350°F) mark 4 and cook for a further 7-10 minutes.
4 Whisk the whole eggs and milk together until they are evenly mixed. Spoon the raisins into the flan and pour in the egg mixture.
5 Bake for 35 minutes or until the custard is just set. Set aside for about 15 minutes before serving warm, or leave to cool completely.

TIP

To test the custard, gently shake the flan: the surface should not wobble. Or press gently on the surface of the custard – if set, it will be quite firm to the touch.

PINEAPPLE AND DATE SALAD
WITH KUMQUATS

PREPARATION TIME 35 minutes, plus chilling
COOKING TIME 15 minutes
FREEZING Not suitable

SERVES 6
- *75 ml (5 tbsp) acacia honey*
- *50 g (2 oz) soft brown sugar*
- *300 ml (10 fl oz) Earl Grey tea, strained*
- *225 g (8 oz) kumquats, halved*

330 CALS/SERVING
- *2 oranges, peeled*
- *1 medium pineapple*
- *12 fresh or dried dates, halved and stoned*
- *125 g (4 oz) walnut halves*

1 First make the syrup. Place the honey, sugar and tea in a saucepan and bring to the boil. Boil for 1 minute. Place the kumquats in the syrup. Simmer, uncovered, for about 10 minutes until the kumquats are tender. Leave to cool in the syrup.
2 Slice the oranges crosswise and place in a bowl. Using a sharp knife, cut the top and bottom off the pineapple and cut away the skin. Quarter the pineapple lengthways and cut out the core. Cut the flesh into large chunks. Carefully mix with the oranges.
3 Stir the dates into the fruit mixture with the walnuts. Drain the kumquats and set aside; strain

the syrup and pour over the fruit in the bowl. Cover and chill for 1 hour.
4 Spoon the fruit salad into a serving dish or individual glass bowls and scatter the kumquats on top. Serve with whipped cream.

NOTE Kumquats are readily available at Christmas and have a sharp perfumed flavour. Some stores sell crystallized kumquats which are ideal for decorating desserts and cakes.

VARIATION Substitute 4 ripe pears for the pineapple and cook the kumquats in a syrup flavoured with jasmine tea rather than Earl Grey.

CLEMENTINES IN BRANDY

PREPARATION TIME 10-15 minutes
FREEZING Not suitable
♡ ⏱

SERVES 6
- *10 clementines or other seedless 'easy peelers'*
- *12 pitted dates or no-soak prunes*
- *juice of 1 lemon*

140 CALS/SERVING
- *30 ml (2 tbsp) caster sugar*
- *60 ml (4 tbsp) brandy*

1 Peel the clementines. Remove as much pith as possible then thickly slice into a bowl. Roughly slice the dates or prunes and stir into the clementines.
2 Stir the lemon juice, sugar and brandy into the fruit. Cover and chill until required.

LIME AND CRANBERRY ICE

PREPARATION TIME 15 minutes, plus freezing
COOKING TIME 5-10 minutes
FREEZING Suitable
❄

SERVES 8
- *550 g (1¼ lb) cranberries*
- *8 egg yolks*
- *225 g (8 oz) caster sugar*
- *450 ml (15 fl oz) milk*

270 CALS/SERVING
- *2 limes*
- *500 g (1 lb 2 oz) carton bio natural yogurt*
- *juice of 1 orange*

1 Place the cranberries in a saucepan with a little water and heat gently until slightly softened. Drain well.
2 Whisk together the egg yolks and 175 g (6 oz) sugar until thick and pale. Bring the milk to just below boiling point, then pour it onto the egg mixture, whisking continuously. Rinse out the saucepan.
3 Return the mixture to the pan and heat gently, stirring, until the custard thickens slightly and just coats the spoon. Do not boil or the custard will curdle. Strain into a large bowl. Leave to cool.
4 Finely grate the rind of both limes and squeeze out 30 ml (2 tbsp) lime juice. Add the yogurt to the custard with 350 g (12 oz) cranberries and the lime rind and juice. Blend in batches in a food processor until almost smooth.
5 Pour into a freezer container to a depth of about 5 cm (2 inches). Freeze for about 4 hours until mushy, then beat well to break down the ice crystals. Freeze again until firm, for at least 8 hours. (If using an ice-cream maker, churn the mixture in the usual way.)
6 Place the remaining cranberries in a pan with the remaining sugar and the orange juice. Place over a gentle heat until the sugar dissolves and the cranberries are heated through. Pour into a bowl and leave to cool. Cover and chill.
7 About 1½ hours before serving, transfer the ice cream to the refrigerator to soften. Serve scoops with the cranberries in syrup.

VANILLA ICE WITH ESPRESSO

PREPARATION TIME 5 minutes
FREEZING Not suitable
🕐

SERVES 6
- *espresso coffee*
- *vanilla or a 'nutty' luxury ice cream*

260 CALS/SERVING
- *chocolate-covered coffee beans or tiny chocolates, to serve*

1 Make up the espresso coffee according to the instructions on your machine.
2 Scoop the ice cream into glasses and pour about 45-60 ml (3-4 tbsp) hot espresso over each serving.
3 Serve with some chocolate-covered coffee beans or tiny chocolates.

TIP
If you don't have an espresso machine, use very strong black coffee or the sachets or jars of instant espresso coffee that can be found in most supermarkets.

RICH CHRISTMAS CAKE

PREPARATION TIME 30 minutes, plus storing and icing
COOKING TIME 2½-3 hours
FREEZING Not suitable

SERVES 12-16

- *150 g (5 oz) each glacé cherries, dried figs, apricots, dates, raisins, sultanas*
- *50 g (2 oz) mixed peel*
- *175 ml (6 fl oz) dark rum*
- *175 g (6 oz) skinned, roasted hazelnuts*
- *225 g (8 oz) butter, softened*
- *grated rind of 1 lemon*
- *225 g (8 oz) soft dark brown sugar*
- *4 eggs, beaten*

610-460 CALS/SERVING

- *30 ml (2 tbsp) black treacle*
- *225 g (8 oz) white plain flour*
- *10 ml (2 tsp) ground mixed spice*

TO COVER

- *60-90 ml (4-6 tbsp) honey or apricot jam*
- *350 g (12 oz) white marzipan*
- *450 g (1 lb) ready-to-roll fondant icing*

TO DECORATE

- *gold ribbon*
- *red and gold berries*
- *gold fir cones*

1 Line a 20 cm (8 inch) round deep cake tin with a double thickness of greaseproof paper.
2 Rinse the glacé cherries to remove all the syrup.

Drain and dry on absorbent kitchen paper. Very roughly chop the cherries, figs, apricots and dates. Mix all the fruit and the mixed peel with 125 ml (4 fl oz) rum and soak for 3-4 hours.
3 Place 50 g (2 oz) hazelnuts in a blender or food processor and blend until finely chopped. Roughly chop the remainder.
4 Beat the butter with the lemon rind until soft and pale in colour. Gradually beat in the sugar until well mixed. Beat in the eggs a little at a time. Beat in the treacle until evenly blended.
5 Sift the flour and spice together and fold half into the creamed ingredients. Stir in all the hazelnuts. Gently fold in all the fruit, followed by the remaining flour. Spoon into the prepared cake tin, then level off the surface. Tie a band of brown paper around the outside of the tin.
6 Bake at 150°C (300°F) mark 2 for 2½-3 hours or until a fine skewer inserted into the centre comes out clean.
7 Pierce the surface with a fine skewer and spoon over the remaining rum. Leave the cake in the tin for 1 hour, then turn out. Cool on a wire rack. Remove all the lining paper and wrap tightly in fresh greaseproof paper and foil. Store in a cool, dry place for at least a week and up to 2 months.
8 To marzipan the cake, warm half the honey or apricot jam with 15 ml (1 tbsp) water in a pan

and brush over the cake. On a surface lightly dusted with icing sugar, roll out the marzipan in a circle, large enough to cover the top and sides of the cake – about 10 cm (4 inches) bigger than the cake top. Place over the cake, press gently around the sides, then trim the edges. Dry for 2 days.

9 To fondant-ice, warm the remaining honey or sieved apricot jam with 15 ml (1 tbsp) water in a pan. Lightly brush over the cake. Sprinkle a work surface and rolling pin with cornflour. Roll out the fondant icing until it is about 10 cm (4 inches) larger than the cake top. Cover the cake. Leave to dry in a cool place for 2 days, covered, then decorate with ribbon, berries and cones.

STOLLEN

PREPARATION TIME 40 minutes, plus rising
COOKING TIME About 40 minutes
FREEZING Suitable

❄

SERVES 10
- *15 g (1/2 oz) fresh yeast or 7 g (1/4 oz) sachet fast-action dried yeast*
- *about 175 ml (6 fl oz) tepid milk*
- *350 g (12 oz) strong white plain flour*
- *5 ml (1 tsp) salt*
- *3.75 ml (3/4 tsp) ground mixed spice*
- *50 g (2 oz) butter*
- *finely grated rind of 1 lemon*
- *25 g (1 oz) caster sugar*

325 CALS/SERVING
- *50 g (2 oz) currants*
- *75 g (3 oz) raisins or sultanas*
- *25 g (1 oz) chopped mixed peel*
- *40 g (1 1/2 oz) flaked almonds*
- *1 egg, beaten*
- *melted butter, for brushing*
- *175 g (6 oz) almond paste or white marzipan*
- *icing sugar for dusting*

1 If using fresh yeast, blend with the milk. Sift the flour, salt and spice into a bowl and rub in the butter. Stir in the lemon rind, sugar, currants, raisins, mixed peel, almonds and fast-action dried yeast, if using. Make a well in the centre of the dry ingredients and add the yeast liquid or milk and egg. Beat to form a soft dough, adding a little more milk if necessary.

2 Turn out the dough onto a floured surface and, with floured hands, knead for 8-10 minutes until the dough is elastic and almost smooth. Place in an oiled bowl. Cover with oiled clingfilm and leave in a warm place for 1 1/2-2 hours until doubled in size.

3 Using floured hands, knock down the dough, then place on a lightly floured work surface and knead for 1-2 minutes only. Roll out the dough to a 25 cm (10 inch) square. Brush lightly with melted butter. Knead and roll out the almond paste to a strip about 23 x 10 cm (9 x 4 inches) and place down the centre of the dough. Fold the dough over the almond paste and seal well.

4 Pinch the ends together to enclose the almond paste. Place, seam-side down, on a buttered baking sheet. Make a few slits across the top. Cover and leave in a warm place for 30-45 minutes until doubled in size.

5 Bake at 190°C (375°F) mark 5 for 40 minutes or until sounding hollow when tapped. Cool on a wire rack. Dust with icing sugar.

MINCE PIES

PREPARATION TIME 1 hour
COOKING TIME About 25 minutes
FREEZING Suitable

❄

MAKES ABOUT 24
- *Shortcrust Pastry, made with 225 g (8 oz) flour (see page 75)*
- *about 225 g (8 oz) Apricot Mincemeat (see page 72)*

105 CALS/MINCE PIE
- *1 egg white, lightly beaten*
- *caster sugar*
- *cream, to serve*

1 Roll out the pastry thinly and cut out about 48 5.5 cm (2 1/4 inch) rounds, re-rolling as necessary.

2 Place half the rounds on baking sheets and spoon mincemeat onto the centre of each. Moisten the pastry edges. Cover with the remaining pastry rounds, sealing the edges well; flute, if wished. Make a hole in the top to allow steam to escape.

3 Bake at 200°C (400°F) mark 6 for about 15 minutes or until just set but not browned.

4 Take out of the oven and brush with lightly beaten egg white and dredge with caster sugar. Return to the oven for a further 8-10 minutes or until well browned. Serve the mince pies warm with cream.

BUCHE DE NOEL

PREPARATION TIME 1 hour
COOKING TIME About 10 minutes
FREEZING Suitable (stage 7)

❄

SERVES 8-10

- *3 eggs*
- *125 g (4 oz) caster sugar*
- *75 g (3 oz) white plain flour*
- *30 ml (2 tbsp) cocoa powder*
- *440 g (15½ oz) can sweetened chestnut purée*
- *icing sugar for dusting*

720-575 CALS/SERVING

- *holly sprigs, to decorate*

BUTTER CREAM

- *225 g (8 oz) unsalted butter*
- *50 g (2 oz) plain chocolate*
- *450 g (1 lb) icing sugar*

1 To make the cake, grease a 33 x 23 cm (13 x 9 inch) Swiss roll tin. Line with greaseproof paper and grease the paper. Dredge with a little caster sugar, then with a little flour, knocking out any excess.

2 Put the eggs and sugar in a deep heatproof bowl and stand it over a saucepan of simmering water. Whisk until thick enough to leave a trail on the surface when the whisk is lifted.

TIP
For an attractive additional decoration, make meringue mushrooms; bake 'caps' and 'stalks' separately and stick together with butter cream.

---

3 Take the bowl off the saucepan and continue whisking the mixture for 5 minutes or until cool. Sift in the flour and cocoa and gently fold into the mixture. Fold in 15 ml (1 tbsp) hot water.

4 Pour the mixture gently into the prepared tin and lightly level the surface. Bake in the oven at 200°C (400°F) mark 6 for about 10 minutes or until slightly shrunk away from the sides of the tin.

5 Meanwhile, place a sheet of greaseproof paper on top of a tea towel. Dredge the paper with caster sugar and turn the cake out onto it. Trim off the crusty edges with a sharp knife. Roll up the cake with the paper inside. Transfer to a wire rack, seam side down, and leave to cool for 20 minutes.

6 To make the butter cream, beat the butter until soft. Put the chocolate with 15 ml (1 tbsp) water in a heatproof bowl over hot water. Melt, then leave to cool slightly. Gradually sift and beat the icing sugar into the softened butter, then add the melted chocolate.

7 Unroll the cold Swiss roll. Remove the paper and spread the chestnut purée over the cake. Roll up again and place on a cake board or plate.

8 Cut a thick diagonal slice off one end of the Swiss roll and attach with butter cream to the side of the roll.

9 Using a piping bag and a large star nozzle, pipe thin lines of butter cream over the log. Pipe one or two swirls of butter cream to represent knots in the wood. Decorate the log with sprigs of holly and dust lightly with icing sugar.

FLORENTINES

PREPARATION TIME 20 minutes, plus cooling
COOKING TIME About 15 minutes
FREEZING Not suitable

MAKES ABOUT 30

- *100 g (3½ oz) butter*
- *125 g (4 oz) caster sugar*
- *125 g (4 oz) flaked almonds, roughly chopped*
- *25 g (1 oz) sultanas*
- *5 glacé cherries, chopped*

120 CALS/SERVING

- *25 g (1 oz) chopped mixed peel*
- *15 ml (1 tbsp) single cream or milk*
- *300 g (10 oz) plain chocolate*

1 Line 4 baking sheets with non-stick baking parchment. Melt the butter in a saucepan over a low heat, add the sugar and boil the mixture for 1 minute.

2 Remove the pan from the heat and add all the remaining ingredients, except the chocolate, stirring well to mix.

3 Drop the mixture into small heaps onto the prepared baking sheets, allowing space between each for the mixture to spread.

4 Bake in the oven at 180°C (350°F) mark 4 for 10-15 minutes or until golden brown.

5 Remove from the oven and press around the edges of the biscuits with the blade of a knife to neaten the shape. Leave on the baking sheets for 5 minutes or until beginning to firm, then cool on a wire rack.

6 When the biscuits are cool, melt the chocolate and leave it to cool for about 10-15 minutes or until it coats the back of a spoon and is just beginning to set.

7 Spread the chocolate over the backs of the biscuits. Mark wavy lines in the chocolate with a fork and leave to set.

VARIATION To make more elaborate florentines, for serving as petits fours, make them slightly smaller than here. Coat half with plain and half with milk chocolate, then pipe with contrasting lines of chocolate to decorate.

SHORTBREAD

PREPARATION TIME 20 minutes, plus chilling
COOKING TIME 20 minutes
FREEZING Not suitable

MAKES 24-36

270-180 CALS/BISCUIT

- *450 g (1 lb) butter*
- *225 g (8 oz) caster sugar*
- *450 g (1 lb) white plain flour*
- *225 g (8 oz) rice flour or ground rice*
- *pinch of salt*
- *golden or coloured granulated sugar, for coating*
- *caster sugar, for sprinkling*

1 Line 2 baking sheets with greaseproof paper. Cream the butter and sugar together in a bowl until pale and fluffy. Sift the flour, rice flour and salt together and stir into the creamed mixture until it resembles breadcrumbs.

2 Gather the dough together with your hand and turn onto a clean work surface. Knead lightly until it forms a ball, then lightly roll into a sausage, about 5-7.5 cm (2-3 inches) thick. Wrap in clingfilm and chill until firm.

3 Unwrap the roll and slice into discs, about 7-10 mm (⅓-½ inch) thick. Pour golden or coloured granulated sugar onto a plate and roll the edge of each disc in the sugar. Place the biscuits, cut-side up, on the baking sheets.

4 Bake at 190°C (375°F) mark 5 for about 15-25 minutes, until very pale golden. Remove from the oven and sprinkle with caster sugar. Allow to cool on the baking sheet for 10 minutes, then transfer to a wire rack to cool.

VARIATIONS *Spiced Shortbread:* Sift 15 ml (1 tbsp) ground mixed spice with the flours.
Ginger Shortbread: Sift 5 ml (1 tsp) ground ginger with the flours. Add 50 g (2 oz) chopped crystallized ginger to the dough.
Chocolate Chip Shortbread: Knead 50 g (2 oz) chocolate chips into the dough.

CRANBERRY AND ROAST SHALLOT CHUTNEY

PREPARATION TIME 25 minutes
COOKING TIME About 40 minutes
FREEZING Not suitable

MAKES 900 G (2 LB)

45 CALS/25 G (1 OZ)

- *450 g (1 lb) shallots*
- *45 ml (3 tbsp) olive oil*
- *225 g (8 oz) soft brown sugar*
- *salt and pepper*
- *450 g (1 lb) cranberries*
- *2.5 cm (1 inch) piece fresh root ginger, peeled and finely grated*

- *15 ml (1 tbsp) mustard seeds*
- *150 ml (5 fl oz) red wine*
- *200 ml (7 fl oz) red wine vinegar*
- *45 ml (3 tbsp) crème de cassis liqueur*

1 Plunge the shallots into a pan of boiling water for 5 minutes to loosen the skins, then remove. When cool enough to handle, carefully peel, leaving on a little root end to hold them intact.
2 Halve the shallots lengthwise and place in a roasting tin with the olive oil and 45 ml (3 tbsp) of the sugar. Roast at 200°C (400°F) mark 6 for at least 30 minutes, turning twice until softened and caramelized, but not burnt. Season generously with salt and pepper.
3 Meanwhile, pick over the cranberries, discarding

any discoloured ones. Place in a heavy-based saucepan with the ginger, remaining sugar, mustard seeds, red wine and vinegar. Bring slowly to the boil and simmer for 10-15 minutes until the cranberries burst and the mixture thickens. Remove from the heat.
4 Stir in the shallots. Deglaze the roasting tin with the liqueur and reduce until syrupy, then pour into the cranberry mixture. Return to the heat and simmer very gently, stirring occasionally, for 10-15 minutes or until the chutney is thick. Pot and cover in the usual way (see page 77).

APRICOT MINCEMEAT

PREPARATION TIME 10 minutes, plus standing
FREEZING Not suitable

MAKES 1.8 KG (4 LB)

45 CALS/15 ML (1 TBSP)

- *225 g (8 oz) no-soak dried apricots*
- *finely grated rind and juice of 1 orange*
- *900 g (2 lb) mixed currants, sultanas and raisins*
- *60 ml (4 tbsp) orange marmalade*

- *450 g (1 lb) demerara sugar*
- *7.5 ml (1½ tsp) ground mixed spice*
- *1.25 ml (¼ tsp) freshly grated nutmeg*
- *300 ml (10 fl oz) brandy*

1 Snip the apricots into small pieces, and mix with the orange rind, 45 ml (3 tbsp) orange juice and all the remaining ingredients.
2 Cover and leave for 48 hours, stirring occasionally.
3 Pot and cover in the usual way (see page 77) and store in a cool place for up to 2 months.

TIP
Make the mincemeat at least a week ahead. Always stir the mincemeat before using as ingredients at the top can become dry.

TANGERINE JELLY MARMALADE

PREPARATION TIME 40 minutes
COOKING TIME About 2¼ hours
FREEZING Not suitable

**MAKES ABOUT 2.3 KG
(5 LB)**
- *900 g (2 lb)
tangerines, washed*
- *1 large grapefruit,
washed*

35 CALS/15 ML (1 TBSP)
- *1 lemon, washed*
- *5 ml (1 tsp) citric
acid*
- *1.4 kg (3 lb) sugar*

1 Peel the tangerines and cut the peel into fine shreds. Tie the shreds in a piece of muslin.
2 Peel the grapefruit and lemon and cut the peel up finely. Roughly chop the flesh of all the fruit, reserving the juice, and put the flesh, juice and peel in a preserving pan with the muslin bag.
3 Add the citric acid and 2.8 litres (5 pints) water to the pan and simmer for about 2 hours or until the fruit is soft. Remove the muslin bag after 30 minutes, squeezing it well and allowing the juice to run back into the pan.
4 Untie the muslin bag, place the tangerine peel in a sieve, wash under cold water, then drain and reserve.
5 Spoon the pulped fruit into a jelly bag or cloth attached to the legs of an upturned stool, and leave to strain into a large bowl for about 2 hours.
6 Discard the pulp remaining in the jelly bag. Pour the extract into a clean preserving pan and add the sugar. Heat gently, stirring, until the sugar has dissolved. Bring to the boil, stir in the reserved tangerine peel and boil rapidly for 10 minutes or until setting point is reached (see page 77).
7 Remove any scum with a slotted spoon, leave the marmalade to stand for 15 minutes, then stir to distribute the shreds. Pot and cover in the usual way (see page 77).

NOTE All together, the unprepared fruit should weigh about 1.3 kg (2¾ lb).

SEVILLE ORANGE MARMALADE

PREPARATION TIME 30 minutes
COOKING TIME About 2½ hours
FREEZING Not suitable

**MAKES ABOUT 4.5 KG
(10 LB)**
- *1.4 kg (3 lb) Seville
oranges*

35 CALS/15 ML (1 TBSP)
- *juice of 2 lemons*
- *2.7 kg (6 lb) sugar*

1 Halve the oranges and squeeze out the juice and pips. Tie the pips, and any membrane that has come away during squeezing, in a piece of muslin. Slice the orange peel thinly or thickly, as preferred, and put it in a preserving pan with the fruit juices, muslin bag and 3.4 litres (6 pints) water.
2 Simmer gently for about 2 hours or until the peel is really soft and the liquid reduced by about half. Remove the muslin bag, squeezing it well and allowing the juice to run back into the pan. Add the sugar. Heat gently, stirring until the sugar has dissolved.
3 Bring to the boil and boil rapidly for 15 minutes until setting point is reached (see page 77).
4 Remove any scum with a slotted spoon. Leave to stand for 15 minutes, then stir to distribute the peel. Pot and cover in the usual way (see page 77).

BASIC RECIPES

Making your own stocks and pastry will give recipes that extra depth of flavour, while homemade mayonnaise and bread will give everyday meals a culinary lift.

VEGETABLE STOCK

PREPARATION TIME 15 minutes
COOKING TIME 1 3/4 hours
FREEZING Suitable

MAKES 1.1 LITRES (2 PINTS)
- *30 ml (2 tbsp) vegetable oil*
- *1 onion, peeled and finely chopped*
- *1 carrot, peeled and diced*
- *50 g (2 oz) turnip, peeled and diced*
- *50 g (2 oz) parsnip, peeled and diced*
- *4 celery sticks, chopped*
- *vegetable trimmings, such as celery tops, cabbage leaves, mushroom peelings, tomato skins*
- *1 bouquet garni*
- *6 black peppercorns*
- *a little salt*

1 Heat the oil in a saucepan, add the onion and fry gently for about 5 minutes until lightly coloured.
2 Add the other vegetables to the pan with the trimmings and 1.7 litres (3 pints) water. Add the bouquet garni and peppercorns. Season with salt.
3 Bring to the boil, partially cover and simmer for 1½ hours, skimming occasionally.
4 Strain the stock and leave to cool. Cover and store in the refrigerator. Use within 1-2 days.

BEEF STOCK

PREPARATION TIME 15 minutes,
COOKING TIME 4½-5½ hours
FREEZING Suitable

MAKES 900 ML (1½ PINTS)
- *450 g (1 lb) shin of beef, cut into pieces*
- *450 g (1 lb) marrow bones or knuckle of veal, chopped*
- *1 bouquet garni*
- *1 onion, peeled and sliced*
- *1 carrot, peeled and sliced*
- *1 celery stick, sliced*
- *2.5 ml (½ tsp) salt*

1 To give a good flavour and colour, brown the meat and bones in the oven before using them. Place in a roasting tin and cook at 220°C (425°F)

mark 7 for 30-40 minutes until well browned.
2 Put the bones and meat in a saucepan with 1.7 litres (3 pints) water, the bouquet garni, vegetables and salt. Bring to the boil and remove any scum.
3 Partially cover and simmer for 4-5 hours.
4 Strain and, when cold, remove all traces of fat.

CHICKEN STOCK

PREPARATION TIME 15 minutes
COOKING TIME 2-3 hours
FREEZING Suitable

MAKES 1.1 LITRES (2 PINTS)
- *1 chicken carcass, bones and trimmings from a roast chicken*
- *1 onion, peeled and sliced*
- *1 carrot, peeled and sliced*
- *1 celery stick, sliced*
- *1 bouquet garni*
- *1 bay leaf*
- *salt*

1 Break up the chicken carcass and put in a large saucepan with any skin and meat attached, plus other bones and trimmings.
2 Add 1.7 litres (3 pints) water, the onion, carrot, celery, bouquet garni, bay leaf and a little salt. Bring to the boil, then skim.
3 Partially cover and simmer for 2-3 hours.
4 Strain and, when cold, remove all traces of fat.

FISH STOCK

PREPARATION TIME 10 minutes
COOKING TIME 20 minutes
FREEZING Suitable

MAKES 900 ML (1½ PINTS)
- *450-750 g (1-1½ lb) fish bones and trimmings*
- *salt*
- *1 bouquet garni*
- *1 onion, peeled and sliced*

1 Put the fish bones and trimmings into a saucepan, cover with 900 ml (1½ pints) water and add a little salt. Bring to the boil, then skim.
2 Reduce the heat and add the bouquet garni and

onion. Cover and simmer for 20 minutes.
3 Strain and leave to cool. Use on the same day, or store in the refrigerator for not more than 2 days.

SHORTCRUST PASTRY

PREPARATION TIME 10 minutes, plus resting
FREEZING Suitable

For shortcrust pastry, the proportion of flour to fat is 2:1, or twice the quantity. Therefore, for a recipe using quantities of shortcrust pastry other than 225 g (8 oz), simply use half the quantity of fat to the flour weight specified.

MAKES 225 G (8 OZ)   175 CALS/25 G (1 OZ)
- *225 g (8 oz) white plain flour*
- *pinch of salt*
- *125 g (4 oz) butter or margarine, chilled and diced*

1 Mix flour and salt together in a bowl. Add the fat to the flour. Using your fingertips, rub the fat lightly into the flour until the mixture resembles fine breadcrumbs.
2 Add 45-60 ml (3-4 tbsp) chilled water, sprinkling it evenly over the surface.
3 Stir in with a round-bladed knife until the mixture begins to stick together in large lumps. Collect the dough mixture together to form a ball.
4 Knead lightly for a few seconds to give a firm, smooth dough; do not overhandle the dough. Wrap in clingfilm or greaseproof paper and rest in the refrigerator for about 30 minutes.
5 To roll out the pastry, sprinkle a very little flour on a work surface and the rolling pin (not on the pastry) and roll out the dough evenly in one direction only, turning it occasionally. The usual thickness is 3 mm (⅛ inch). Do not pull or stretch the pastry.

VARIATION *Walnut Shortcrust Pastry* Follow the recipe for Shortcrust Pastry, stirring in 40 g (1½ oz) very finely chopped, shelled walnuts before adding the water.

BAKING BLIND

If a recipe for a flan or tart instructs you to bake blind, it means that you should partially or completely bake the pastry case before filling. To bake blind, first prick the pastry base with a fork, then line with a large piece of greaseproof paper or foil. Fill with ceramic baking beans or dried pulses. Small cases don't need lining – just prick with a fork.

For partially baked cases, bake at 200°C (400°F) mark 6 for 10-15 minutes until the case looks 'set'. Carefully remove the paper or foil and the beans and bake for a further 5 minutes until the base is firm to the touch and lightly coloured.

For completely baked cases, return to the oven for about 15 minutes until firm and golden brown.

PUFF PASTRY

PREPARATION TIME 40 minutes, plus resting
FREEZING Suitable

The richest of all the pastries, puff requires patience, practice and very light handling. Whenever possible it should be made the day before use. It is not practical to make in a quantity with less than 450 g (1 lb) flour weight. This quantity is equivalent to two 375 g (13 oz) packets.

MAKES 450 G (1 LB)   270 CALS/25 G (1 OZ)
- *450 g (1 lb) strong plain flour*
- *pinch of salt*
- *450 g (1 lb) butter or margarine, chilled*
- *15 ml (1 tbsp) lemon juice*

1 Mix the flour and salt together. Cut off 50 g (2 oz) of the butter and flatten the remaining butter with a rolling pin to a slab 2 cm (¾ inch) thick.
2 Cut the 50 g (2 oz) butter into small pieces, add to the flour and rub in. Using a round-bladed knife, stir in the lemon juice and about 300 ml (10 fl oz) chilled water to make a soft, elastic dough.
3 Quickly knead the dough until smooth and shape into a round. Cut through half the depth in the shape of a cross. Open out to form a star.
4 Roll out, keeping the centre four times as thick as the flaps. Place the slab of butter in the centre.
5 Fold the flaps envelope-style and press gently with a rolling pin. Roll out to a rectangle measuring about 40 x 20 cm (16 x 8 inches).
6 Fold bottom third up and top third down, keeping the edges straight. Seal edges. Wrap in greaseproof paper and rest in the refrigerator for 30 minutes.
7 Put the pastry on a lightly floured work surface with the folded edges to the sides, then repeat the rolling, folding and resting sequence 5 times.

PATE SUCREE

PREPARATION TIME 10 minutes, plus resting
FREEZING Suitable

Pâte Sucrée is the classic French rich short pastry used for sweet flans.

MAKES 125 G (4 OZ)
- *125 g (4 oz) white plain flour*
- *pinch of salt*
- *50 g (2 oz) butter (at room temperature)*

255 CALS/25 G (1 OZ)
- *2 egg yolks*
- *50 g (2 oz) caster sugar*

1 Sift the flour and salt onto a work surface. Make a well in the centre and add the butter, egg yolks and sugar.
2 Using the fingertips of one hand, pinch and work the sugar, butter and egg yolks together until well blended.
3 Gradually work in all the flour to bind the mixture together. Knead lightly until smooth, then wrap the pastry in clingfilm and leave to rest in a cool place for at least 30 minutes. Roll out as for Shortcrust Pastry (see page 75).

SWEET FLAN PASTRY

PREPARATION TIME 10 minutes, plus resting
FREEZING Suitable

This is made by the same method as shortcrust pastry, but beaten egg is used instead of water.

MAKES 125 G (4 OZ)
- *125 g (4 oz) white plain flour*
- *pinch of salt*
- *75g (3 oz) butter or margarine, chilled and diced*

250 CALS/25 G (1 OZ)
- *5 ml (1 tsp) caster sugar*
- *1 egg, beaten*

1 Sift the flour and salt into a bowl. Rub in the fat until the mixture resembles fine breadcrumbs. Stir in the sugar.
2 Add the egg, stirring with a round-bladed knife until the ingredients begin to stick together.
3 With one hand, form into a firm, smooth dough. Wrap the pastry in clingfilm and rest in a cool place for at least 30 minutes. Roll out as for Shortcrust Pastry (see page 75).

WHOLEMEAL BREAD

PREPARATION TIME 30 minutes, plus rising
COOKING TIME 35 minutes
FREEZING Suitable

MAKES 1 LOAF
- *15 g ($\frac{1}{2}$ oz) fresh yeast or 7 g sachet (1$\frac{1}{2}$ tsp) fast-action dried yeast*
- *150 ml (5 fl oz) tepid milk*
- *450 g (1 lb) wholemeal plain flour*

1700 CALS/LOAF
- *5 ml (1 tsp) salt*
- *5 ml (1 tsp) caster sugar*
- *25 g (1 oz) butter or margarine*
- *beaten egg, water or milk for glazing*

1 If using fresh yeast, blend with the milk. Mix the flour, salt and sugar in a bowl, and stir in the fast-action dried yeast if using. Rub in the butter. Make a well in centre and pour in the yeast liquid or milk and about 175 ml (6 fl oz) tepid water. Mix to a soft dough.
2 Turn out the dough onto a lightly floured surface and knead for about 10 minutes until smooth and elastic. If using fresh yeast, place in an oiled bowl and cover with oiled clingfilm. Leave to rise until doubled in size and sponge-like.
3 Knock the risen dough down, then knead again on a lightly floured surface for 3-4 minutes until smooth. Flatten the dough to an oblong the length of a 900 g (2 lb) loaf tin but three times as wide. Fold in three, turn over, then place in the lightly greased tin.
4 Cover the dough with oiled clingfilm and leave to rise in a warm place for about 45 minutes, or until the dough has risen to the rim of the tin.
5 Brush with beaten egg, water or milk to glaze. Bake at 220° C (425° F) mark 7 for 20 minutes. Reduce the temperature to 180° C (350° F) mark 4 and remove the bread from the tin. Bake for a further 15 minutes. To test, tap the bottom crust; the bread should sound hollow. Cool on wire rack.

NOTE Dough made with fast-action dried yeast only requires one rising. Glazing with beaten egg produces a deep golden shiny finish; brushing with water gives a crisp crust; milk produces a soft, golden crust.

VARIATION *Soft White Bread:* Use strong white plain flour with 200 ml (7 fl oz) tepid milk and 75 ml (3 fl oz) tepid water.

MAYONNAISE

PREPARATION TIME 10-15 minutes
FREEZING Not suitable

MAKES 150 ML (5 FL OZ)
- *1 egg yolk*
- *2.5 ml (½ tsp) mustard powder or 5 ml (1 tsp) Dijon ·mustard*
- *2.5 ml (½ tsp) salt*
- *1.25 ml (¼ tsp) pepper*

140 CALS/15 ML (I TBSP)
- *15 ml (1 tbsp) white wine vinegar or lemon juice*
- *about 150 ml (5 fl oz) oil*

1 Put the egg yolk in a bowl with the mustard, seasoning and 5 ml (1 tsp) of the vinegar or lemon juice. Mix thoroughly.
2 Add the oil drop by drop to begin with, then in a steady stream, whisking constantly, until the sauce is thick and smooth. If it becomes too thick, add a little more vinegar or lemon juice.
3 When all the oil has been added, add the remaining vinegar or lemon juice gradually and mix thoroughly. Store for up to 3 days in the refrigerator.
NOTE Never use eggs straight from the refrigerator as this may result in curdling.

PRESERVING TIPS

Making your own jams, jellies, chutneys and other preserves is one of the most satisfying ways of storing abundant seasonal fruit and vegetables. To achieve the best results, there are certain points about the process you should bear in mind.

PRESERVING EQUIPMENT

If you make a lot of preserves, it's worth investing in a proper preserving pan; the sloping sides help maintain a fast boil and reduce the chances of everything boiling over. Choose a pan made from stainless steel, tin-lined copper or lined aluminium. Don't use unlined aluminium.

If you don't have a preserving pan use a large heavy-based saucepan instead. Note that if you are using a saucepan rather than a preserving pan the preserve will take much longer to reach the setting point owing to the reduced surface area.

For jelly making, you will need a jelly bag for straining the juice from the cooked fruit. Although you can improvise with a large piece of muslin, a jelly bag is a worthwhile investment because it makes things easier. Whatever you use, it should be scalded with boiling water before use. If the jelly bag doesn't have a stand, suspend it from the legs of an upturned chair or stool.

TESTING FOR A SET

Jams, jellies, marmalades and conserves are cooked sufficiently when setting point is reached. There are various tests to determine this. Remove the pan from the heat while you are testing, to prevent overcooking.

Temperature test: The preserve is ready when the temperature registers 105°C (221°F) on a sugar thermometer.
Saucer test: Drop a spoonful of the preserve onto a chilled saucer and leave to cool. Push your finger through the jam; if the surface wrinkles, the preserve is ready.
Flake test: Using a wooden spoon, lift a little of the preserve out of the pan. Let it cool slightly then tip the spoon so that the preserve drops back into the pan; if the drips run together and fall from the spoon in a 'flake' rather than as drips, it is ready.

There is no accurate test for chutneys and pickles, because they are not cooked to a setting point. Instead, be guided by the consistency and cooking time specified in the recipe; they are ready when the mixture is very thick.

POTTING PRESERVES

All preserves should be potted into scrupulously clean containers. Wash jars or bottles in really hot soapy water, rinse thoroughly, then dry in a warm oven. Stand them upside down on a clean tea towel until the preserve is ready. Aim to pour hot jam or marmalade into the jars while they are still warm, to reduce the chances of the glass cracking, and fill them almost to the top. If potting jam, jelly, marmalade or conserve, cover with a waxed disc while the preserve is piping hot or else completely cold, then seal with a dampened clear disc secured with an elastic band. If you seal while the preserve is warm, mould will grow on the surface. Chutneys and pickles are covered in the same way. For long-term storage, cover the jar with a screw top as well.

FREEZING

Freezing is an easy and convenient way to preserve fresh food, allowing you to save and store for later use the wealth of seasonal delicacies that are available fresh for only a short time of the year. Whether you freeze ingredients in their basic state or made up into complete dishes, you will find a well-stocked freezer an invaluable help for producing nutritious meals with the minimum of fuss - especially if you also own a microwave for rapid thawing and reheating.

TIPS FOR EFFICIENT FREEZING

• Freeze only food of the best quality. Never freeze food that looks blemished or old.
• Handle the food as little as possible.
• Never put any foods that are still slightly warm into the freezer, as a rise in temperature causes frosting up and deterioration of other foods will result.
• Never freeze more than one tenth of your freezer's capacity in any 24 hours, as this will also cause the internal temperature to rise.
• When freezing large quantities, use the fast-freeze option.
• Pack and seal food with care. If moisture or cold air is allowed to come into contact with the food it will begin to deteriorate. Cross flavouring might also occur.
• Be sure to wrap non-packaged foods well before freezing. Solid foods must be packaged tightly, with as little air as possible. Wrap items in foil or freezer film; ordinary clingfilm is not suitable for the freezer. Freezer film can also be used as a lining for acidic foods which should then be over-wrapped in foil.
• Where possible use square containers to store food in the freezer; they stack better than round ones and therefore waste less space.
• Interleave any items of food that might otherwise stick together with pieces of greaseproof paper, polythene, foil or freezer film.
• When freezing liquids always leave room for expansion, as frozen liquid expands by about one-tenth of its volume and will push the lids off containers that have been overfilled.
• Freeze single and double portions for easy use.
• Keep you freezer as full as possible. If necessary add loaves of bread to fill up spaces. Empty spaces require more energy to keep cool.
• Make sure food is clearly labelled and dated.

Always use up old stocks first. To help you do this it is a good idea to keep a freezer log book, adding items (with the date) as you freeze them and deleting them as they are consumed.
• Do not re-freeze food once it has been thawed, unless it has been subsequently cooked.
• Check your freezer is operating correctly with a freezer thermometer. It should read -18°C (0°F).

FREEZER STORAGE CHART

This chart is a guide to approximate maximum storage times for certain types of food. Always follow the manufacturer's instructions.

VEGETABLES
blanched vegetables (most types) 10-12 months
mushrooms and tomatoes 6-8 months
vegetable purées 6-8 months

FRUIT
fruit in syrup 9-12 months
open frozen fruit 6-8 months
fruit purées 6-8 months
fruit juice 4-6 months

FISH
white fish 6-8 months
oily fish 3-4 months
fish portions 3-4 months
shellfish 2-3 months

MEAT AND POULTRY
beef and lamb 4-6 months
pork and veal 4-6 months
offal 3-4 months
sliced bacon/other cured meat 2-3 months
ham and bacon joints 3-4 months
chicken and turkey 4-6 months
duck and goose 4-6 months
venison 4-6 months
rabbit and game 4-6 months
sausages, sausagemeat 2-3 months
minced beef 3-4 months

PREPARED FOOD
soups and sauces 3 months
stock 6 months
prepared meals 4-6 months
    if highly seasoned 2-3 months
bread 2-3 months

pastries 3-4 months
cakes 4-6 months

DAIRY PRODUCE
cream 6-8 months
butter (salted) 3-4 months
cheese (hard) 4-6 months
cheese (soft) 3-4 months
ice cream, mousses etc 3-4 months

FREEZER EMERGENCIES

The most common freezer emergency is loss of power. This can be as a result of a power cut or someone inadvertently turning the freezer off. If there is a power cut, don't panic; if you leave the freezer door closed the food should stay frozen for about 30 hours (48 hours in a chest freezer). If possible, wrap the freezer with a blanket to increase insulation.

If you have advance warning of a power cut, turn on the fast-freeze switch, making sure the freezer is full to capacity. Towels or rolled newspaper can be used to fill any gaps.

Do not re-freeze any food you suspect may have begun to thaw.

FREEZING FRESH VEGETABLES

Vegetables can be very successfully frozen, but only if they are really fresh - no more than 12 hours after they were picked. Blanching the vegetables before freezing will help to preserve their colour, flavour and texture.

To blanch vegetables, bring a large pan of water to the boil and immerse the vegetables up to 450 g (1 lb) at a time. Bring back to the boil and keep the vegetables immersed for the required time - delicately textured or leafy vegetables such as spinach, mangetout and sliced courgettes will only need about 10 seconds, while firmer varieties such as broccoli and cauliflower florets, green beans and peas will need to be blanched for 1 minute. Root vegetables like carrots should be sliced and blanched for 2-3 minutes, while whole dense vegetables like globe artichokes and small beetroot need 4-5 minutes.

Once blanched, immediately remove the vegetables and plunge into a bowl of iced water. The blanching water can be used 6-7 times and the iced water refreshed with more ice as necessary. The vegetables can be put into a blanching basket for this part of the operation, but if you do not have one a suitable strainer or a large piece of muslin will do.

FREEZING FRESH FRUIT

First, check that the fruit you wish to freeze is properly ripe and in peak condition, free from any blemishes. Any overripe fruit should be puréed before freezing. With fruits such as apples you will have to cook them first before puréeing, but fruits such as peaches and raspberries can be puréed in their fresh form.

Before freezing the fruit, consider how it will eventually be used. Small fruits which do not need peeling are best frozen as they are; remove any stalks if necessary, and open freeze by spreading them on trays lined with non-stick paper, then transfer to polythene bags. They will not stick together, enabling small quantities to be removed as needed.

Firm fruits and any which have a tendency to discolour should be frozen in a syrup made with 450 g (1 lb) sugar to 1 litre (1³/₄ pints) water and the juice of 1 lemon. The fruits can be left whole, halved or sliced into the cool syrup as appropriate. For fruits such as grapefruit and pineapple omit the lemon juice and substitute any juice from the fruit.

THAWING FROZEN FOOD

Thawing must be done thoroughly and efficiently to ensure food is safe to eat.
• Never leave food to thaw in a warm environment; this is the ideal breeding ground for harmful bacteria. Instead, let the food thaw gradually in the refrigerator or in a cool larder.
• Cover food loosely while thawing.
• Make sure large items such as joints of meat are thoroughly thawed before cooking. The legs of poultry should be able to move freely.
• Dispose of any liquid which seeps from thawing meat and poultry. Do not allow it to come into contact with other food.
• Cook food as soon as possible after it is thawed.
• If thawing frozen food in a microwave, follow the manufacturer's instructions.
• Only use the microwave if you plan to eat or cook the food immediately.

INDEX